REPORT OF THE DIRECTOR-GENERAL

TIME FOR EQUALITY AT WORK

Global Report
under the Follow-up to the ILO Declaration
on Fundamental Principles and Rights at Work

INTERNATIONAL LABOUR CONFERENCE
91st Session 2003

Report I (B)

INTERNATIONAL LABOUR OFFICE
GENEVA

This Report may also be consulted on the ILO Internet site
(http://www.ilo.org/declaration).

ISBN 92-2-112871-7
ISSN 0074-6681

First published 2003

Second impression 2004

Photocomposed by the International Labour Office, Geneva, Switzerland
Printed in Switzerland

DTP
ATA

Contents

Executive summary

Discrimination in one form or another occurs in the world of work every day, throughout the world. At the same time, work is a privileged entry point from which to liberate society from discrimination. This is the key message of this Report.

Literally millions of people in the world are denied jobs, confined to certain occupations or offered lower pay simply because of their sex, their religion or the colour of their skin, irrespective of their capabilities or the requirements of the job. At its worst, the discrimination that certain groups, such as women, ethnic or racial minorities and migrants, face in the labour market makes them vulnerable to such abuses as forced or compulsory labour. Barriers to decent jobs often compel parents belonging to an ethnic minority or a denigrated caste to resort to the labour of their children to make ends meet. Discrimination at work deprives people of their voice at work and full participation, thus undermining democracy and justice in the workplace.

The elimination of discrimination at work is essential if the values of human dignity and individual freedom, social justice and social cohesion are to go beyond formal proclamations. *Time for equality at work* is the fourth Global Report under the follow-up to the ILO Declaration on Fundamental Principles and Rights at Work. It examines the diverse forms of discrimination at work that have been identified and formally condemned nationally and internationally. It gives an update of the various policy and practical responses, with the aim of mobilizing greater support for the elimination of discrimination in respect of employment and occupation.

The elimination of discrimination is essential if all individuals, irrespective of their physical or cultural traits and beliefs, are to be able to choose freely the direction of their professional paths and working lives, to develop fully their talents and capabilities and to be rewarded according to merit.

Time for equality at work argues that the benefits of eliminating discrimination in the workplace transcend the individual and extend to the economy and to society. Workers who enjoy equal treatment and equal opportunities improve the efficient use of human resources and diverse talents. This improves workforce morale and motivation, leading to better labour relations with positive implications for overall productivity. A more equal distribution of job opportunities, productive resources and assets, including education, between men and women of different races, religions or ethnic origins, contributes to higher growth and political stability. The elimination of discrimination at work is an indispensable component of any strategy for poverty reduction and sustain-able development. It lies at the heart of the ILO's mandate and the notion of decent work.

The workplace, be it a factory, an office, a plantation, a farm or the street, is a strategic entry point from which to combat discrimination in society. People who are denied equal opportunities, equal treatment and dignity at work often suffer discrimination in other spheres as well. In the workplace, however, discrimination can be tackled more readily and effectively. By bringing together people of different race, sex, age, national extraction and physical ability and treating them fairly, the workplace helps to defuse prejudices and shows that social life and activity free of discrimination is possible, effective and desirable.

Discrimination at work will not vanish by itself; neither will the market, on its own, take care of its elimination. The elimination of discrimination requires deliberate, focused and consistent efforts and policies by all parties concerned, over a sustained period of time. It is not only the duty of governments to combat discrimination, it is everybody's responsibility. Enterprises, employers' and workers' organizations and the victims of discrimination and their associations all have both a stake and a role to play in achieving equality at work.

Part I of the Report retraces the growth of the awareness that discrimination in employment and occupation, in its different forms, is intolerable. This is true especially for racial and sex-based discrimination, where the world has moved from ignorance or denial to awareness and remedial action. The Report reviews some of the milestones since the Second World War in the international recognition of discrimination and commitment to its elimination. The mobilization and organization of people experiencing discrimination has been the primary force to challenge entrenched stereotypes and prejudices and to elicit national and international public policy responses. In this global movement, the ILO has pioneered international consensus and provided policy guidance on how to tackle discrimination at work.

Racism was the form of discrimination that first galvanized the international community. The ILO Constitution cried out for action against apartheid regimes, and the Discrimination (Employment and Occupation) Convention, 1958 (No. 111), provided a policy framework for eliminating all forms of discrimination at work. In 1964, the International Labour Conference initiated action against the policy of apartheid implemented by the Government of South Africa.

The other major form of discrimination that has attracted the attention of the international community since the Second World War is discrimination based on sex, and discrimination against women in particular. Through the guarantee of "equal remuneration for work of equal value", the Equal Remuneration Convention, 1951 (No. 100), introduced a radically innovative concept – already affirmed in the ILO Constitution – that allows examination of the gender biases in labour market structures. More recently, discrimination based on other grounds, such as age, disability, perceived or actual HIV/AIDS status and nationality has raised similar concerns and has led to increased national and international action.

While some of the more blatant forms of discrimination may have faded, many remain, and others have taken on new or less visible forms. Changes in the structure and dynamics of labour markets, which stem from broader political, economic and cultural processes, redefine patterns of social stratification and social mobility. They produce new manifestations of discrimination that, in turn, generate new inequalities. For example, the combined effect of global migration, the redefinition of national boundaries in some parts of the world, and growing economic problems and inequalities have exacerbated problems of xenophobia and racial and religious discrimination.

The Report traces the boundaries of discrimination at work. It demonstrates that discrimination in employment and occupation is a complex and moving target. Perceptions, rather than objective facts, about the abilities and attitudes ascribed to individuals belonging to certain social groups can give rise to discrimination in the labour market. Perceptions are shaped by the values prevailing in society at different times. The entrenched nature of discrimination often renders it invisible, and hence difficult to combat. It is difficult in practice, especially with the more subtle forms of discrimination, to determine the extent to which equal rights and opportunities are denied. There is an absence of data on the extent to which direct or indirect discrimination affects the situation of individuals in their daily work.

Discrimination at work may manifest itself in access to a job, while performing a job or, indeed, through dismissal from a job. Individuals who face discrimination in access to a job tend to continue experiencing discrimination while in the job, in a vicious cycle of cumulative disadvantage. *Time for equality at work* argues that discrimination at work does not result just from isolated acts of an employer or a worker or from a single policy measure. Rather, labour market processes, practices and institutions either generate and reinforce, or break the cycle of discrimination. Institutions and practices are not set in stone, and they can be changed to promote equality.

Part II examines gender disparities in labour force participation rates, unemployment rates, remuneration and the jobs performed by most women and most men, within the serious limitations of the data available on the extent of the different forms of discrimination. These data are generally regarded as valid approximations for ascertaining discrimination at entry to the labour market and in a job. The Report shows that while there has been some progress, such instances of eliminating sex-based discrimination are not irreversible, and much more needs to be done. While women's participation in the labour market and, more importantly, in non-agricultural wage employment has increased almost everywhere, unemployment rates have generally been higher for women than they have for men. In the 1980s and 1990s, the range of occupations in which women were employed broadened in a majority of countries, especially in some OECD countries and in several small developing countries where occupational segregation was high. The opposite trend was observed in some transition economies. It appears, however, that as horizontal segregation declines, vertical segregation often tends to rise.

With regard to remuneration, although the gender gap has been decreasing in most places, it is still large. Pay differentials between men and women have been narrowing in Latin America and in the OECD countries, although at a slow pace. Women's lower educational attainments and intermittent career paths are not, contrary to conventional belief, the main reason for gender differentials in pay. Other factors, such as occupational segregation, biased pay structures and job classification systems, and decentralized or weak collective bargaining, appear to be more important determinants of inequalities in pay. The Report raises the question of whether a minimum wage policy would help to reduce pay differentials at the bottom end of the pay structure, as women and groups that are discriminated against, such as migrant workers or members of ethnic minorities, are disproportionately represented in low-paid jobs.

Different policy issues and responses are considered in Part II. The patterns and structure of inequality differ according to the country, and they are as varied as the perceptions of what is considered intolerable, and also according to the financial and human resources available at different stages of socio-economic development. Despite these differences, and while responses can be only country-specific, *Time for equality at work* shows that whatever the form of discrimination – be it based on race, sex, age, disease or disability – its elimination tends to require a similar set of policy devices. These range from consistent and effective regulatory and institutional frameworks to suitable training and employment policies. What can be changed is the combination of policies, as can the relative weight of each policy instrument at different stages.

A common trend is a shift from laws that prohibit discrimination to laws that provide for a positive duty to prevent discrimination and promote equality. These seem to be more effective in tackling the subtlest forms of discrimination, such as occupational segregation. Processes of economic and political integration, such as the European Union, have helped to harmonize legislation in this field. Public policy, beyond legislation, is also helpful in addressing discrimination at work: for example, public procurement policies can be a powerful device to combat discrimination at work against members of minority groups or persons with disabilities.

Effective enforcement, monitoring and promotional institutions are needed for anti-discrimination laws to be effective. The challenges for enforcement are manifold, ranging from understaffing to staff with little expertise and effective authority. However, many countries are working to meet these challenges by enhancing remedies and sanctions, streamlining procedural rules and making labour inspections more effective. A universal feature is the establishment of specialized bodies to tackle discrimination and promote equality at work. Their powers, structures and composition differ. They may focus on one single group, such as women or minority groups, or they may deal with various grounds of discrimination at the same time. There appears to be a tendency, especially in developed countries, to support the establishment of institutions dealing with a variety of forms of discrimination simultaneously.

Time for equality at work argues that affirmative action measures are necessary to ensure that everyone can start on an equal footing. This is true especially when socio-economic inequalities between groups are profound and stem from past and societal discrimination. While education is instrumental for access to decent jobs, returns to education tend to be lower for members belonging to groups that are discriminated against. Hence, an anti-discrimination strategy that focuses exclusively on ensuring equal access to education would not suffice; supportive labour market and other socio-economic policies are essential.

Part III considers the work of the ILO and of the social partners in eliminating discrimination. Action by the social partners, with whom the Office works closely, depends on two primary conditions. The right of workers and employers to organize in democratic and representative organizations must be guaranteed. Their members and their organizational activities should be free from any discrimination. At the same time, both employers' and workers' organizations have a prime responsibility to identify and to recognize existing discriminatory practices, and to combat these through all their activities – starting from within their own organizations. In situations where employers' and workers' organizations wish to expand their membership and the scope of collective bargaining, an equality agenda can become a window of opportunity for their growth and vitality. The chapter on this subject provides examples of how discrimination can be overcome by the social partners, how collective bargaining can be a conduit for equality and how enterprises can recognize the value of equality for their business.

The principle of eliminating discrimination runs through much of the normative work of the ILO, influencing the labour legislation assistance that the Office has provided to constituents for developing equality-oriented legal frameworks. Operational programmes and projects for eliminating discrimination have been directed at specific groups such as women, migrant workers, workers with disabilities, including HIV/AIDS, and indigenous and tribal peoples.

Following its path-breaking contribution to the defeat of apartheid in South Africa and the establishment of the new democratic regime, the ILO has furthered its work on gender issues. With regard to discrimination based on sex, there has been a progressive shift from focusing exclusively on women – from homeworkers to managers and entrepreneurs – towards gender mainstreaming. While activities have been concentrated on removing barriers to employment and upward occupational mobility, more needs to be done to reduce inequalities in vocational training and in wages and other terms and conditions of work. At the same time, other forms of discrimination also require greater attention. This calls for innovative and responsive approaches to help overcome cultural and political sensitivities relating to discrimination based on race, religion and political opinion.

In Part IV, the Report outlines a plan of action for addressing discrimination at work, to facilitate the efforts of the tripartite constituents to find appropriate solutions. Where work is already being carried out, dissemination of information and experience should help make this work and its results better known. Where particularly important gaps have been identified, ILO action needs to be strengthened. The capacity of member States and the social partners to deal with the multiple facets of discrimination should be strengthened and supported.

An effective action plan could be based on three strategies – *knowledge*, *advocacy* and *services* – that provide the starting point from which to implement the three main lines of action. Under *knowledge*, the plan proposes the development of "equality-at-work indicators" as an element of decent-work indicators. This would assist governments and their social partners in drawing up "road maps" to see where they stand with regard to discrimination on different grounds and to help then progress towards the elimination of these forms of discrimination.

The people who suffer from discrimination tend to be those in the poorest segments of society, yet anti-poverty strategies seldom address the link between poverty and systemic discrimination. With an enhanced knowledge base on this link, the ILO would be better placed to promote non-discriminatory policies and labour market institutions for targeting poverty, as part of a rights-based approach in the Poverty Reduction Strategy Papers and the United Nations Development Assistance Framework processes.

A major test of any attempt to eliminate discrimination at work is how it addresses wage inequalities. The ILO should document the extent of discrimination in remuneration in order better to assess the real extent of pay discrimination based on sex, race, national origin and other grounds. To understand and address this discrimination, "equal pay tool-kits" could be part of broader wages and human resources policies.

Under *advocacy*, the plan proposes a sustained information and awareness-raising effort that would highlight cases where discrimination has been successfully eliminated. Such a sustained effort would address a broad range of people, from political decision-makers to local community groups, and illustrate, in particular through information from the tripartite constituents of the ILO, who are the primary agents for promoting equality at work and, how work can be a strategic entry point for practical ways to prevent and eliminate discrimination and to promote equality.

And finally, under *services*, the plan proposes to strengthen traditional ILO assistance in drafting or revising legislation relating to equality. It also seeks to strengthen national capacity to enforce this legislation. This requires two types of action. One relates to the need for traditional labour market institutions to address equality concerns on a regular and informed basis. The other concerns the need to establish or strengthen national institutions dedicated to promoting and monitoring equality. A facility could be set up to assist in the establishment and operation of such institutions with mandates relating to equality.

While discrimination is now universally condemned, and progress towards equality of opportunity and treatment has been made, there is clearly a long way to go. Greater determination by all will help us reach the goal of eliminating discrimination. The ILO constituents are the primary parties with a responsibility to work to eliminate discrimination in the workplace, and they also draw the benefits of success. Separately and together, and with such assistance as the ILO can offer both now and in the future, they should take matters in hand to realize progressively the Declaration's principle of the elimination of discrimination in respect of employment and occupation. This Report strongly encourages them to take steps in this direction. It also reiterates the commitment of the ILO to increase its support to achieve this common target.

Introduction

1. Discrimination occurs in the world of work every day, throughout the world. There is discrimination every time a worker is shunned or preferred because of the colour of his or her skin, or when a competent woman manager is denied a seat in the boardroom or paid less than a male colleague with equal productivity. There is discrimination every time a pregnancy test is required for a woman to be considered for a job, or when a mineworker is dismissed because of perceived or actual HIV/AIDS status. And there is discrimination every time a business licence is denied to an entrepreneur because of his or her religion, or when a woman is required to obtain the approval of her spouse to get a bank loan.

Discrimination – a worldwide problem

2. Discrimination in employment and occupation takes many forms, and occurs in all kinds of work settings. But all discrimination shares a common feature. It entails treating people differently because of certain characteristics, such as race, colour or sex, which results in the impairment of equality of opportunity and treatment. In other words, discrimination results in and reinforces inequalities. The freedom of human beings to develop their capabilities and to choose and pursue their professional and personal aspirations is restricted, without regard for ability. Skills and competencies cannot be developed, rewards to work are denied and a sense of humiliation, frustration and powerlessness takes over.

Common features of discrimination

3. Society at large is also profoundly affected. The waste of human talent and resources has a detrimental effect on productivity, competitiveness and the economy; socio-economic inequalities are widened, social cohesion and solidarity are eroded and political stability comes under threat.

4. The elimination of discrimination at work is central to social justice, which lies at the heart of the ILO's mandate. It underpins the concept of decent work for all women and men, which is founded on the notion of equal opportunities for all those who work or seek work and a living, whether as labourers, employers or self-employed, in the formal or the informal economy. The elimination of discrimination is an indispensable part of any viable strategy for poverty reduction and sustainable economic development.

Elimination of discrimination is central to social justice

5. The Declaration of Philadelphia, adopted by the International Labour Conference in 1944 and now part of the ILO Constitution, recalls that "all human beings, irrespective of race, creed or sex, have the right to pursue both their material well-being and their spiritual development in conditions of freedom

and dignity, of economic security and equal opportunity". Equality at work is a constant theme in the international labour standards adopted and promoted by the ILO. It is the subject of two of the eight fundamental Conventions:[1] the Discrimination (Employment and Occupation) Convention, 1958 (No. 111), and the Equal Remuneration Convention, 1951 (No. 100). These are among the most widely ratified ILO Conventions (see Annex 2).

6. The ILO Declaration on Fundamental Principles and Rights at Work and its Follow-up, adopted in June 1998, reaffirmed the constitutional principle of the elimination of discrimination in respect of employment and occupation, thereby confirming the universal resolve to suppress discrimination in the world of work through the promotion of equal treatment and opportunity.

Proactive approaches

7. In recent decades, countries have adopted laws against discrimination and have undertaken proactive approaches to eliminate unequal treatment at work. Enterprises and employers worldwide have modified recruitment and hiring procedures and practices, wage-setting systems and management policies to ensure fairness at work. Trade unions have made equality their goal in collective bargaining and in other actions, as well as in their internal representative structures. Today, we are aware of the multiple links between discrimination and poverty, social exclusion and forced and child labour. Our understanding of how to tackle these problems has improved, but there is still a long way to go before discrimination at work is a thing of the past.

8. As a phenomenon, discrimination in employment and occupation is both universal and constantly changing: it is a moving target. Some of the most blatant forms of discrimination have faded away; however, many still remain or have taken on new forms. In many cases, discrimination has acquired more subtle, less visible forms. Changes in the structure and dynamics of labour markets, which stem from broader political, economic and cultural processes, redefine patterns of social stratification and social mobility. They produce new manifestations of discrimination.

9. A thorough understanding of discrimination at work and regular monitoring of its manifestations and social and economic consequences are required if decent work[2] deficits are to be eliminated. In the light of changes in the sex, age and ethnic composition of the world labour force and labour markets, a full-employment strategy has to have an inclusive approach to employment and work. Equal opportunities provide the indispensable avenue for achieving this goal.

10. The voices of all workers and employers who are discriminated against need to be heard, including those in the informal economy and those not engaged in wage labour. Basic freedoms such as freedom of association and freedom from forced or child labour help underpin action against discrimination.

The workplace – a strategic entry point

11. The workplace – be it a factory, an office, a plantation, a farm or the street – is a strategic entry point to free society from discrimination. When the work-

---

[1] The Forced Labour Convention, 1930 (No. 29), the Freedom of Association and Protection of the Right to Organise Convention, 1948 (No. 87), the Right to Organise and Collective Bargaining Convention, 1949 (No. 98), the Equal Remuneration Convention, 1951 (No. 100), the Abolition of Forced Labour Convention, 1957 (No. 105), the Discrimination (Employment and Occupation) Convention, 1958 (No. 111), the Minimum Age Convention, 1973 (No. 138) and the Worst Forms of Child Labour Convention, 1999 (No. 182).

[2] Decent work is the converging focus of the four strategic objectives: the promotion of rights at work; employment; social protection; and social dialogue. The primary goal of the ILO today is to promote opportunities for women and men to obtain decent and productive work, in conditions of freedom, equity, security and human dignity. ILO: *Decent work*, Report of the Director-General, International Labour Conference, 87th Session, Geneva, 1999, p. 3. See also ILO: *Reducing the decent work deficit: A global challenge*, Report of the Director-General, International Labour Conference, 89th Session, Geneva, 2001.

place brings together people with different characteristics and treats them fairly, it helps to combat stereotypes in society as a whole. It forces a situation where prejudices can be defused and rendered obsolete. A socially inclusive world of work helps to prevent and to redress social fragmentation, racial and ethnic conflict and gender inequalities.

12. If the capacity to deal efficiently with discrimination in the workplace is not strengthened, it will be more difficult to face the challenges arising out of increases in internal and external migration, unprecedented technological change, transition to market economies with their rapidly shifting groups of winners and losers, and the need to accommodate and reconcile a variety of languages, cultures and values. This may well be the most challenging task of contemporary society, and it is essential for social peace and democracy.

13. This is the first Global Report on the elimination of discrimination in employment and occupation. It is the last in the first four-year cycle of Global Reports under the follow-up to the ILO Declaration on Fundamental Principles and Rights at Work.[3] The Report focuses on those aspects of discrimination at work that, in the light of recent trends, warrant special attention today. This is either because of their persistence, their scale, their potential effects in the foreseeable future, or because neglecting them will have disastrous effects on national social cohesion, political stability, and hence growth. The Report also seeks to identify what, in practice, the ILO can, and should, do better to avoid negative consequences and to promote protection for the women and men who are daily subject to discrimination.

The scope of the Global Report

14. Part I of the Report examines discrimination in employment and occupation. It traces changes in the extent, characteristics and dynamics of the problem and its perception.

15. Part II focuses on selected trends and issues. Using the data available on reasons for discrimination – which are often limited or even non-existent, except for discrimination on the basis of sex – it analyses patterns and trends in occupational segregation and differentials in remuneration between women and men, and it reviews national public policies to combat discrimination.

16. Part III reviews the work of the ILO to address the issue of discrimination, including the policy approaches, strategies and means of action, as well as initiatives by employers' and workers' organizations and enterprises.

17. Finally, Part IV outlines a number of suggestions on how the relevance and effectiveness of the ILO could be increased. In particular, it invites a debate on the type of plan of action that could benefit ILO member States and employers' and workers' organizations in their endeavours to overcome discrimination at work.

Priorities for future ILO action

---

[3] The ILO Declaration applies to all member States of the ILO, whether or not they have ratified the Conventions relating to each category of principles concerning fundamental rights. Under the follow-up to the Declaration, a Global Report is to be drawn up each year under the responsibility of the Director-General and to cover one of the four categories of fundamental principles and rights in turn. The Global Reports may be consulted on the ILO Internet site http://www.ilo.org/declaration

Part I. From principle to reality

1. Growing international recognition of the need to eliminate discrimination in the world of work

18. Society typically seems to follow an approach to discrimination that ranges from ignorance or denial to remedial action. In between, there is the important stage of awareness of discrimination, which may lead to recognition of the problem and its implications.

19. Part I of the Report seeks to present a picture of discrimination at work in its different forms, from the above perspective. While there have been important cases of progress in this respect, there is no irrevocable linear movement from ignorance to remedial action. Different countries are at different stages along this spectrum. Not only do they vary according to the different forms of discrimination, but they also vary according to the type of remedial action they take. Raising and maintaining awareness and remaining alert to the shifting nature of the manifestations of discrimination are essential.

Different forms of discrimination at work

The ILO: A key player in building international consensus

20. To discriminate in employment and occupation is to treat people differently on the basis of race, colour or sex, among other reasons, irrespective of their capabilities or the requirements of the job. Perceptions and stereotypes are heavily influenced by history, economic and social situations, political regimes and the cultural background of countries. Perceptions and prejudices, and tolerance or intolerance towards discriminatory practices, are shaped by the values that prevail in society at different times. At the same time, values and principles evolve, and social movements and institutions play a key role in lowering individuals' and societies' tolerance towards discriminatory behaviour and practices.

Perceptions and stereotypes

21. Thus, it is important to review how the international community has come to agree on the need to eliminate discrimination and to promote equality in the world of work, and to examine the factors that have contributed to this process. Our review will naturally place ILO standard-setting activities within the proper social and political perspectives. In this way, we can outline the major

grounds for, and areas of, discrimination, which will subsequently be developed in greater detail in Chapters 2 and 3.

Racism and racial discrimination

22. Racism and racial discrimination were the first forms of discrimination that preoccupied the international community. Racism has been and still is at the heart of the most outrageous social tragedies. Although slavery and the slave trade had been outlawed by the late 1800s, the extraction of forced and compulsory labour from native populations by colonial administrations was still widespread in the 1920s. This led the League of Nations to adopt the Slavery Convention in 1926. The ILO adopted the Forced Labour Convention, 1930 (No. 29), which called for each Member of the ILO to undertake "to suppress the use of forced or compulsory labour in all its forms within the shortest possible period" (Article 1(1)). As the colonial era approached its end, concern emerged with respect to the use of forced labour for ideological reasons or as a means of racial, social, national or religious discrimination. The Abolition of Forced Labour Convention, 1957 (No. 105), made explicit the link between forced labour and "racial, social, national or religious discrimination" (Article 1(c)).

23. The 1950s and 1960s marked a period of intense standard-setting activities, both in the ILO and at the United Nations, on issues relating to the principles of non-discrimination and equality in the world of work and beyond. Today, the Equal Remuneration Convention, 1951 (No. 100), and the Discrimination (Employment and Occupation) Convention, 1958 (No. 111), are among the most widely ratified of all the ILO Conventions (see Annex 2). They were the first instruments with the specific aim of promoting equality and eliminating discrimination in the world of work. They have also influenced the drafting of subsequent and related United Nations Conventions.

24. The inclusion of "race" in Convention No. 111 as unacceptable grounds for discrimination reflected international consensus and commitment to combat racism, which had been signalled by the 1948 Universal Declaration of Human Rights. The horror at the Holocaust, in which millions died because they belonged to a certain race, was acute. Questions of racism and racial discrimination, including segregation, continued to attract and elicit renewed international and national responses during the 1950s and 1960s. The end of colonialism revealed the challenges and problems of unequal development arising from the consequences of regimes that were now being dismantled. Through the International Convention on the Elimination of All Forms of Racial Discrimination, adopted by the United Nations in 1965, the expanding international community – many developing countries had now joined the United Nations – reiterated its condemnation of racism. At the same time, the civil rights movement in the **United States** achieved the suppression of discriminatory legislation against Americans of African descent in the labour market and beyond, and altered perceptions and attitudes towards them. With the civil rights movement, African Americans themselves led political efforts to improve their situation.

25. But the scourge of racially segregated societies was still alive in other countries, such as **South Africa** and **Namibia**, with **Zimbabwe** (formerly Rhodesia) becoming, in 1980, the first to accept democracy and majority rule.

Action against apartheid

26. The ILO Constitution amply legitimized action against the apartheid regime in **South Africa** and **Namibia**, while Convention No. 111 provided the policy framework. In 1964, the International Labour Conference "acting as a spokesman of the social conscience of mankind", condemned the policy of apartheid implemented by the Government of **South Africa** as contrary to the Declaration of Philadelphia. The ILO Programme for the Elimination of Apartheid in Labour Matters in the Republic of **South Africa** was unanimously adopted, prompting that country to withdraw from the ILO for the next 30 years.

This programme monitored action against apartheid. ILO action evolved from initial recommendations to an unwilling Government to mobilization of opinion against policies of apartheid and the promotion of a policy of isolation of the Government of **South Africa**, until it abolished apartheid. Through this programme, the ILO mobilized material and political support for the national liberation movements and ultimately for the democratic trade unions and employers' organizations acting against apartheid.

27. In 1973, the United Nations adopted the International Convention on the Suppression and Punishment of the Crime of Apartheid, which made apartheid a crime under international law. In 1974, the **South African** delegates were excluded from the United Nations General Assembly deliberations. ILO experience in combating racial segregation in **South Africa** and **Namibia** revealed the strategic importance of eliminating discrimination in the labour market to achieve racial equality in society.

28. Another major form of discrimination that has attracted the attention of the international community since the Second World War is discrimination based on sex, and discrimination against women in particular. Women entered the labour market in large numbers during the Second World War to counter shortages in the labour supply of men, who were engaged in fighting at the front. When the men returned from war, women's presence in the labour market came to be seen as a threat to men's employment and to the overall quality of working conditions. It was feared that women's cheaper labour would restrict the number and range of jobs available to men and, at the same time, condemn women to less important occupations and, at worst, to exploitative conditions of work.

Discrimination based on sex

29. In this case, too, the ILO was in the vanguard. The notion of equal pay for work of equal value had already been enshrined in the ILO Constitution of 1919. Three decades later, Convention No. 100 affirmed the importance of equality between men and women in respect of remuneration, which included the basic wage and any additional cash or in kind remuneration or benefit arising out of the worker's employment. A pioneering feature of this Convention was its guarantee of equal pay for "work of equal value" and not just for the same or similar work. This addresses gender biases in the way labour markets are structured, because most women do different jobs from most men. This principle was subsequently adopted by the European Community Equal Pay Directive in 1975,[1] and by the United Nations Convention on the Elimination of All Forms of Discrimination against Women in 1979.

Gender equality

30. The International Labour Conference also promoted gender equality through the adoption of other documents, including, in 1975, the ILO Declaration on Equality of Opportunity and Treatment for Women Workers and the resolution concerning a plan of action with a view to promoting equality of opportunity and treatment for women workers, which reinforced the commitment of the international community in this respect. This Declaration stressed that, while equality for women was inextricably linked to improvements in the general conditions of work of all workers, all forms of discrimination on the grounds of sex should be eliminated. The relevant policy documents were forwarded to the First World Conference on Women, held in Mexico in 1975, as the ILO contribution to the International Women's Year.

---

[1] Council of the European Communities: Council Directive 75/117/EEC of 10 February 1975 on the approximation of the laws of the Member States relating to the application of the principle of equal pay for men and women.

31. The Workers with Family Responsibilities Convention, 1981 (No. 156), which addresses the problems that these workers, and women in particular, face in the labour market, is a reflection of the ILO's commitment to furthering gender equality at work and in other spheres. Concern about the negative consequences that the unequal sharing of family responsibilities between men and women could have for women's status in society had previously been expressed by the United Nations Convention on the Elimination of All Forms of Discrimination Against Women.

Poverty perpetuated

32. The 1960s and 1970s were marked by a growing concern with poverty, which was particularly serious in countries that had recently been emancipated from colonial regimes. The role of the ILO has been important in showing that poverty was not a residual legacy or accidental in any way but that it was related to the functioning of economic and social institutions.[2] Discrimination and labour market segmentation were powerful mechanisms that perpetuated poverty, as members of certain groups were altogether excluded from the labour market or allowed in only under disadvantaged conditions.[3]

Discrimination-free employment policies

33. The Employment Policy Convention, 1964 (No.122), provides a framework to guide policy interventions aimed at the elimination of poverty and the promotion of development through discrimination-free employment policies. This Convention provides that an active national policy be designed "to promote full, productive and freely-chosen employment" (Article 1(1)), and that it must guarantee the "opportunity for each worker to qualify for, and to use his skills and endowments in, a job for which he is well suited, irrespective of race, colour, sex, religion, political opinion, national extraction or social origin" (Article 1(2c)). The notion of productive employment is based on the realization that no society can afford to waste the talents and abilities of any of its members.

Problems of development and social inequalities

34. The 1990s has witnessed a significant revival of concern with the persistence of poverty. The end of the Cold War, democratization and the opening of global markets did not automatically solve problems of development and social inequalities. In 1995, the World Summit for Social Development, held in Copenhagen, identified the elimination of poverty as priority number one on the international development agenda. It took up the ILO's recognition of the importance of full and productive employment, free from discrimination, to reduce poverty and bring about sustainable and sustained development. Improvements in both the quantity and quality of jobs were deemed to be compatible with efficiency goals, as part of a new search for a balance between efficiency and equity. The Copenhagen World Summit also recorded for the first time consensus on the contents of fundamental workers' rights.

Millenium Development Goals

35. The Millennium Development Goals (MDGs), adopted by the United Nations General Assembly in 2000, set targets to guide national government action towards the reduction of poverty. The share of women in wage employment in the non-agricultural sector has been identified as an indicator to

---

[2] In particular, with the work of the World Employment Programme (WEP) in the 1970s. Many of these issues were raised in the ILO International Institute for Labour Studies' contribution to the 1995 World Summit for Social Development, see G. Rodgers (ed.): *New approaches to poverty analysis and policy – I: The poverty agenda and the ILO: Issues for research and action* (Geneva, ILO/IILS, 1995) and G. Rodgers and R. van der Hoeven (eds.): *New approaches to poverty analysis and policy – III: The poverty agenda: Trends and policy options* (Geneva, ILO/IILS, 1995). ILO work on poverty continues today through, among other things, inputs into the Poverty Reduction Strategy Papers process.

[3] J.B. Figueiredo and Z. Shaheed (eds.): *New approaches to poverty analysis and policy – II: Reducing poverty through labour market policies* (Geneva, ILO/IILS, 1995).

assess the extent to which the goals of gender equality and women's empowerment are achieved. This reflects the importance of women's access to paid jobs in sectors other than agriculture for the improvement of their economic and social status. It confirms the relevance of the ILO's work, including its international labour standards, in removing the obstacles that many women still face in acquiring market-relevant skills and well-remunerated jobs.

36. Concerns about vulnerable and disadvantaged groups have permeated ILO standard-setting and employment and social policies. The protection of the interests of workers employed in countries other than their own has been a major concern of the ILO since its foundation, as reflected in the Preamble of its Constitution and in the Migration for Employment Convention (Revised), 1949 (No. 97), and the Migrant Workers (Supplementary Provisions) Convention, 1975 (No. 143). The 1998 ILO Declaration on Fundamental Principles and Rights at Work reaffirmed the need for the Organization to pay special attention to the needs of migrant workers. A general discussion will be held during the session of the International Labour Conference in 2004 to assess the means available to the ILO to ensure respect for the rights of migrant workers.

Vulnerable and disadvantaged groups

37. The situation of indigenous and tribal peoples has been another matter of concern for the ILO. Shortly after its creation, the Organization dealt with what were then referred to as "native workers" in the context of forced and compulsory labour. Research had revealed that people under colonial domination were most likely to be subject to these abusive work practices. The Indigenous and Tribal Populations Convention, 1957 (No.107), and the Indigenous and Tribal Peoples Convention, 1989 (No. 169), are still the only international legal instruments dealing with the rights of indigenous and tribal peoples.

Indigenous and tribal peoples

38. The discrimination and disadvantages faced by older workers have been addressed by the Organization in the Older Workers Recommendation, 1980 (No. 162), which deals with some of the barriers that these workers face in finding a job or in re-entering the labour market and recommends that working time and social security matters take account of the special needs of older workers. The opportunities and challenges of a rapidly ageing population, a "demographic revolution without precedent", were the themes debated at the Second World Assembly on Ageing held in Madrid in April 2002. The Madrid International Plan of Action on Ageing recognizes the potential of older workers to contribute to development and calls on governments to take urgent action to increase the participation of older workers in the labour force and to provide life-long learning and education.[4] This echoes the ILO position that full employment and integrated policies throughout workers' lives are key to achieving a "society for all ages".

Special needs of older workers

39. The situation of other groups, such as people with disabilities and people living with HIV/AIDS, is gaining increasing attention at international level, including at the ILO. A code of practice on HIV/AIDS and the world of work was approved by consensus at a tripartite meeting of experts from all regions and formally launched, in June 2001, at the United Nations General Assembly Special Session on the subject. This code of practice emphasizes the need to combat discrimination against workers with actual or perceived HIV/AIDS status. In October 2001, the ILO became one of the eight co-sponsors of the Joint United Nations Programme on HIV/AIDS (UNAIDS). ILO concern with

People with disabilities, people with HIV/AIDS

---

[4] Report of the Second World Assembly on Ageing (2002), available at http://www.un.org/esa/socdev/ageing/waa/ and Governing Body doc. GB/285/ESP/6/1, paras. 1, 9 and 10.

this pandemic builds upon long-standing concern with other forms of disability at work. The Vocational Rehabilitation and Employment (Disabled Persons) Convention, 1983 (No. 159), and the Vocational Rehabilitation and Employment (Disabled Persons) Recommendation, 1983 (No. 168), help people with disabilities to have equal access to gainful employment. More recently, a Tripartite Meeting of Experts in Geneva in October 2001 adopted a code of practice on managing disability in the workplace.

Social mobilization and organization: The drive behind international recognition and commitment

40. The mobilization and organization of people experiencing discrimination has been the primary force that has challenged entrenched stereotypes and prejudices and stirred national and international public policy responses.

Identity politics

41. Since the late 1960s, the black and women's movements, indigenous and tribal organizations, the lesbian and gay movements, and organizations – sometimes trade unions – representing people with disabilities and disadvantage have mobilized to seek and obtain recognition of the equal dignity and worth of these people. Identity politics have revolved around demands for political recognition and accommodation of the various social groups in all spheres of society, including in employment and occupation.

Information technology revolution

42. The information technology revolution[5] has accelerated the process of change in people's thinking, perceptions, attitudes and ideas and has enhanced the impact of media on shaping prevalent values (see box 1.1). The free flow of information has had two contradictory effects. In some cases, it has affected the sensitivities of certain groups who may feel that their cultures and ways of life are being challenged by globalization and cosmopolitanism. This fear translates into the rejection of foreign values and the assertion of narrow identities that exacerbate manifestations of xenophobia and expressions of religious or cultural intolerance. The new forms of communication have also engendered new forms of solidarity and cooperation within and across countries. Women's mobilization and collective action in its multiple shapes and orientations, including international and national trade unions, have been able to make use of networking and alliance-building within and across national boundaries. This process has significantly promoted the internationalization of fundamental human values, principles and rights, including freedom from discrimination in employment and occupation.

Human-rights-based approach

43. The 1990s have accelerated the acceptance of, and commitment to, a human-rights-based approach to development. The values and principles in this normative framework are both enabling and empowering. This is recognized for instance in the World Bank's new approach to poverty reduction, where "voicelessness" and "powerlessness" as dimensions of poverty have been introduced. Its approach to empowerment of the poor includes eliminating discrimination on the basis of gender, ethnicity, race and social origin.[6]

---

[5] The "information technology revolution" refers to the ability to process and disseminate data and images at low cost and high speed, breaking down spatial and temporal barriers, see M. Castells: *The information age: Economy, society and culture. Vol II. The power of identity* (Malden, MA, Blackwell, 1997).

[6] World Bank: *Entering the 21st century: World Development Report 2000/2001* (Washington, DC, Oxford University Press, 2001).

Box 1.1

The media: A special responsibility in addressing discrimination

The media reflect our world. They are part of society and are imbued with the same attitudes, intolerance and prejudices. At the same time, they reflect our aspirations for equality and they can voice the concerns of people discriminated against who otherwise would have no voice. In the information age, the impact of the media is fundamental; so is their potential to fight discrimination. How can we detect and combat subtle or blatant forms of discrimination channelled through the media? How can we best make use of the media to promote equality and value diversity? Media representation of social groups tends to be all too often stereotypical. In Europe, the news about ethnic, cultural and religious minorities and migrants tends to over-emphasize ethnic and immigrant crime. Stereotypes about the Roma and Muslims are among the most pernicious. Language and labelling can be a subtle channel to convey subliminal discriminatory messages, which impact on collective imagery. Once a negative discourse misrepresenting migrants or ethnic minorities is established, it tends to prevail. These negative representations are not adequately compensated by positive images, such as the cultural contribution of migrants and other minorities. Conversely, episodes of racism and anti-racism are rarely covered, and mostly when political or other controversy and conflict is involved. Little attention is given to more generalized practices of discrimination and xenophobia, and how to overcome them.

Stereotypical representation occurs equally in portraying gender relations. Not only are women in the media outnumbered by men in a general sense, they are also especially unlikely to be featured as authorities, experts or spokespersons. Women portrayed in the media are younger, more likely to be shown as married, and less likely to be shown in paid employment. The characterization of women in power remains somewhat stereotypical: for example, women's power in the workplace is achieved at the expense of domestic failure. Competing demands of private and public life are presented as problematic for women but not for men.

Today, the media make reference to human rights in their coverage more often and more systematically. Journalists and editors have a professional duty to report and explain human rights issues. However, much reporting focuses on violations of rights during conflicts, while less visibility is given to economic, social and cultural rights, including non-discrimination at work.

Sources: European Research Centre on Migration and Ethnic Relations (ERCOMER): *Racism and cultural diversity in the mass media: An overview of research and examples of good practice in the EU Member States, 1995-2000* (Vienna, 2002); European Commission: *Images of women in the media: Report on existing research in the European Union* (Luxembourg, 1999); International Council on Human Rights Policy: *Journalism, media and the challenge of human rights reporting: Summary* (Versoix, 2002), see www.ichrp.org/excerpts/45.pdf

44. Various United Nations conferences during the 1990s testify to the international commitment to promote equality through a rights-based approach to development. The World Conference on Human Rights, held in Vienna in 1993, forged international consensus that democracy, development and human rights were interdependent and mutually reinforcing and identified target groups for the protection and promotion of human rights. The Vienna Conference also recognized the core labour standards of the ILO as an integral part of human rights. The proclamation of the International Decade of the World's Indigenous People (1995-2004) is another expression of this consensus. The United Nations Fourth World Conference on Women, held in Beijing in 1995, acknowledged that gender equality was a development goal in its own right, and that women's empowerment was essential to achieve this goal: the Beijing Declaration and Platform for Action recognizes that the elimination of

discrimination against women in employment and occupation and the promotion of equal opportunities for women are critical to combat gender inequalities in society. The central role of the workplace in the elimination of all forms of discrimination has also been recognized in other United Nations conferences, including the World Summit for Social Development (Copenhagen, 1995) and the Beijing+5 Women 2000: Gender Equality Development and Peace for the 21st Century (New York, 2000).[7] More recently, the World Conference against Racism, Racial Discrimination, Xenophobia and Related Intolerance (Durban, 2001) confirmed that the creation of workplaces that are representative and respectful of the racial, ethnic and religious diversity of society is indispensable to productivity gains and to generate an overall climate of tolerance and pluralism.

---

[7] The report of the Conference specifically calls on member States to "respect, promote and realize the principles contained in the Declaration on Fundamental Principles and Rights at Work of the International Labour Organization and its follow-up, and strongly consider ratification and full implementation of International Labour Organization Conventions which are particularly relevant to ensuring women's rights at work", para. 94(b).

2. Discrimination: What should be eliminated and why?

What is discrimination?

45. To discriminate in employment and occupation is to treat people differently and less favourably because of certain characteristics, such as their sex, the colour of their skin or their religion, political beliefs or social origins, irrespective of their merit or the requirements of the job (see box 2.1). Discrimination limits the freedom of individuals to obtain the type of work to which they aspire. It impairs the opportunities of men and women to develop their potential, skills and talents and to be rewarded according to merit. Discrimination at work produces inequalities in labour market outcomes and places members of certain groups at a disadvantage.

Discrimination limits the freedom of individuals

46. Perceptions, rather than objective facts, about the abilities or attitudes ascribed to individuals belonging to a particular group can generate discrimination in the workplace and in the labour market. The personal characteristics that give rise to discriminatory behaviour are manifold and they have tended to increase over time.

47. Convention No. 111 (see box 2.1) allows considerable flexibility to ratifying countries in identifying new unlawful grounds of discrimination. Government reports submitted to the ILO under article 22 of the Constitution and article 19, on which the follow-up to the Declaration is based,[8] refer, among other things, to cases of discrimination in employment and occupation based on disability, marital status, state of health, including HIV/AIDS, sexual orientation and trade

---

[8] Article 22 of the ILO Constitution requires each member State "to make an annual report to the International Labour Office on the measures which it has taken to give effect to the provisions of Conventions to which it is a party". The follow-up to the Declaration is based on reports requested from member States under article 19, para. 5(e) of the ILO Constitution, which establishes the reporting procedure for the fundamental Conventions which have not been ratified. According to article 19, member States "shall report ... the position of their law and practice in regard to the matters dealt with in the Convention, showing the extent to which effect has been given, or is proposed to be given, to any of the provisions of the Convention ... and stating the difficulties which prevent or delay the ratification of such Convention".

Box 2.1

Discrimination (Employment and Occupation) Convention, 1958 (No. 111) and its accompanying Recommendation (No. 111)

Scope of application

Convention No. 111 protects all workers against discrimination "on the basis of race, colour, sex, religion, political opinion, national extraction, social origin", and other criteria "as may be determined by the Member concerned after consultation with representative employers' and workers' organisations".

This protection applies to all sectors of employment and occupation, both public and private, and extends to:

— access to education, vocational guidance and training;
— access to employment and occupation (i.e. to work, whether self-employment, wage employment or in the public service);
— access to placement services;
— access to workers' and employers' organizations;
— career advancement;
— security of job tenure;
— collective bargaining;
— equal remuneration for work of equal value;
— access to social security, welfare facilities and benefits related to employment; and
— other conditions of work including occupational safety and health, hours of work, rest periods, holidays.

Definition of discrimination

Discrimination is defined as "any distinction, exclusion or preference made on the basis of race, colour, sex, religion, political opinion, national extraction or social origin, which has the effect of nullifying or impairing equality of opportunity and treatment in employment or occupation" (Article 1(1a)).

What does this definition imply?

■ The presence of intent is not necessary to identify a situation of discrimination.
■ Both direct and indirect discrimination are covered: what matters is the effect of deprivation or limitation of equal opportunity and treatment arising from a difference in treatment.

Measures that do not constitute discrimination include measures based on the inherent requirements of a particular job, measures intended to safeguard the security of the State, and special measures of protection (e.g. to address the specific health needs of women or men) or assistance (e.g. affirmative action and accommodation measures).

The development of a national policy to promote equality

States must establish and implement a national policy to promote equality of opportunity and treatment in employment and occupation with a view to eliminating discrimination. This policy applies to both the public and the private sectors, as well as to vocational guidance, vocational training and placement services under the control of national authorities. States are required to cooperate with workers' and employers' organizations in the preparation and implementation of national policy. These organizations, in turn, must promote national policy in the workplace and within the organization itself.

The State, according to the specific national circumstances, determines which measures are to be developed for the promotion of equal opportunity and treatment. The law and collective agreements are key instruments. Educational activities are a further means to foster the observance of national policy. Moreover, the elimination of certain forms of discrimination may require affirmative action measures.

Box 2.2

Discrimination based on trade union membership

The first Global Report, *Your voice at work,* pointed out that 23 per cent of the allegations examined by the ILO Committee on Freedom of Association concerned acts of anti-union discrimination.[1]

Anti-union discrimination refers to acts that: (i) make access to work or retention of a job subject to the condition that a worker does not join a trade union or relinquish trade union membership; and (ii) cause the dismissal or transfer of a worker because of union membership or because of his/her participation in trade union activities. Since early 2000, the Committee has continued to examine cases where it has found that anti-union discrimination has taken place for a variety of reasons. The cases involve anti-union harassment by public authorities (Panama), sometimes involving interference and intimidation (Belarus, Ukraine), as well as by employers (Bahamas, El Salvador, Romania, Guatemala). Pressure has been exerted on trade union members to leave the union (Paraguay). Several cases have concerned the termination of employment of a trade union leader (Colombia, Guatemala, Morocco, Nicaragua, Peru, Thailand). Employment contracts have not been renewed for anti-union reasons (Turkey). Disciplinary measures have been taken against trade union members following a strike (Haiti, Morocco).

[1] ILO: *Your voice at work,* Report of the Director-General, International Labour Conference, 88th Session, Geneva, 2000, p. 26, figure 2.1.

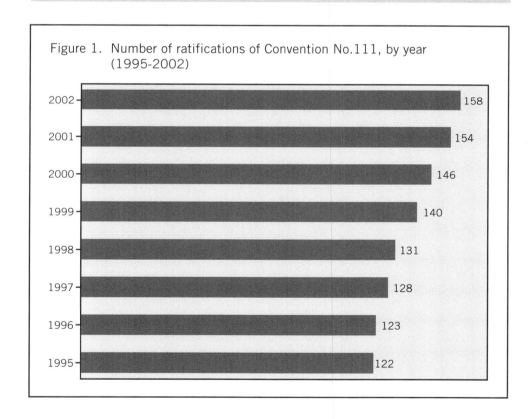

Figure 1. Number of ratifications of Convention No.111, by year (1995-2002)

union membership (see box 2.2), which are not mentioned in Convention No. 111.[9] This Convention is one of the most widely ratified ILO Conventions (see figure 1), and more ratifications are expected. According to information

---

[9] ILO: *Equality in employment and occupation,* Report III(4B), International Labour Conference, 75th and 83rd Sessions (Geneva, 1988 and 1996) and Governing Body docs. GB.277/3/1, GB.280/3/1 and GB.283/3/1.

provided to the Office, the ratification process has been initiated in **Comoros, Djibouti** and the **United States**. Other countries, including **China, Japan, Kiribati, Lao People's Democratic Republic, Oman, Solomon Islands** and **Thailand**, are currently examining the Convention with a view to ratification.

Discrimination in employment and occupation: What work situations are covered?

An inclusive approach

48. Discrimination in the labour market and in the workplace can be found in different work situations and forms of employment in all economic sectors, regardless of whether the work takes place in the formal or the informal economy. Employees in large high-tech businesses, wage earners in informal enterprises, lawyers, farmers and the self-employed may all suffer from discrimination in one form or another. The reference to both employment and occupation means protection from discrimination is provided not only to employees but also to other segments of the labour force, such as own-account workers, owners of enterprises and unpaid family workers. This inclusive approach reflects the recognition that the patterns of economic activity of a country are linked to its stage of economic development. In particular, the relatively high incidence of own-account work is characteristic of many developing countries.

A vicious cycle of cumulative disadvantage

49. Discrimination at work may manifest itself in access to a job and/or while performing a job. People may be excluded or discouraged from even aspiring to a job because of their race, sex or religion. People with disabilities or older workers tend to face tremendous difficulties in obtaining a job or re-entering the labour market after leaving a job. Long-term unemployment may affect members of disadvantaged groups in a society more than it affects other groups. Normally, individuals who face discrimination in access to a job tend to continue experiencing discrimination while in the job, in a vicious cycle of cumulative disadvantage.

50. For other workers, access to employment may not be the main issue. Instead, obstacles may arise with respect to skill development opportunities and career advancement. Preferential demand for female labour relative to male labour in the textile and garment industries in export processing zones is an often-cited example. In this case, more jobs for women are normally not accompanied by either enhanced security of tenure or better career prospects.

Under-representation of certain groups

51. The under-representation of certain groups in vocational training programmes or in enterprise-level skill upgrading schemes reveals the existence of impediments to the acquisition or development of market or enterprise-relevant skills. In **France**, for instance, some vocational training institutions state that they have had difficulties in convincing enterprises to accept trainees of North-African descent. A factor that discouraged these institutions from attracting applications from foreign trainees or trainees of North-African descent was the belief that their reputation would suffer considerably as a result.[10]

Discrimination in remuneration

52. Discrimination also occurs when some individuals who have equivalent skills and performance characteristics or who are performing jobs of equal value are paid less than others because of their sex or their race. For instance,

---

[10] Ministry of National Education: *Discrimination dans l'accès aux stages en entreprise* [Discrimination in access to training in enterprises], speech by Mr. Jean-Luc Mélenchon, Minister with special responsibility for vocational training, during the session on questions to the Government, National Assembly, 1st Session, Paris, 14 June 2000.

a nurse who has degree-level qualifications, has five years' experience in the job and supervises up to 15 people may earn around 30 per cent less than a craft supervisor who has completed joinery apprenticeship, has three years' experience in the job and supervises two people. We shall deal with this question of discrimination in remuneration in more detail in Part II, Chapter 1.

53. The refusal to allow a peasant woman to own or inherit the land she farms is an illustration of discrimination in access to particular occupations. For example, in **Lesotho**, as in many other African countries, women do not have the right of landownership.[11] The refusal to allow women to own land not only impinges upon women's ability to work as farmers, it also limits access to credit and cooperative membership, as both often require landownership. Women's restricted access to agricultural extension services is another impediment to productivity enhancement, and hence to higher incomes. In **Viet Nam**, while women account for nearly 50 per cent of the total agricultural labour force and for a large share in the total number of new jobs created annually in agriculture, they make up only 10 per cent of the beneficiaries of cultivation extension services.[12]

No right of landownership

54. In some instances, the law may restrict women's access to certain occupations. More often, it is social rules and customs that limit the range of jobs available to women. In **Kuwait**, for example, women have limited access to judicial careers, particularly to careers as court judges, because of considerations linked to tradition or religion and not to legislative prohibition.[13]

55. Discrimination at work can also be compounded by violence – either physical or psychological – such as bullying, mobbing or sexual harassment (see box 2.3), against certain categories of workers, thereby affecting their ability to retain a job or progress in that job.

Types of discrimination

56. Discrimination at work can be direct or indirect. Discrimination is direct when regulations, laws and policies explicitly exclude or disadvantage workers on the basis of characteristics such as political opinion, marital status or sex. The prohibition, in some Central and Eastern European countries, for persons who have served in certain functions or bodies of the previous political system to hold jobs in the public sector is a case of direct discrimination based on political opinion. Job advertisements that exclude or overtly discourage applications from married workers or people over a certain age or of a certain colour/complexion are other examples of direct discrimination. Prejudices and stereotypes are normally at the heart of direct discrimination (see figure 2). "Stereotyping" is the process that assigns people particular attitudes and talents or lack of talent, by virtue of their membership in a group, be

Direct discrimination

---

[11] D. Tajgman and E. Kalula: "Analysis of the legal framework for gender equality in employment: Lesotho, a case study", in E. Date-Bah (ed.): *Promoting gender equality at work: Turning vision into reality for the twenty-first century* (London and New York, Zed Books Ltd., 1997), pp. 173-188.

[12] Socialist Republic of Vietnam: *The Comprehensive Poverty Reduction and Growth Strategy* (CPRGS), approved by the Prime Minister at Document No. 2685/VPCP-QHQT, dated 21 May 2002, para. 3.6.

[13] Observation in a direct request concerning Convention No. 111 made by the Committee of Experts on the Application of Conventions and Recommendations to the Government concerned at its 71st Session (Geneva 2000), unpublished document.

Box 2.3

Sexual harassment

Sexual harassment in the workplace is any unwanted sexual attention that is explicitly or implicitly made a condition for favourable decisions affecting one's employment or that creates an intimidating, hostile or offensive work environment. It is a specific form of violence that concerns primarily, but not exclusively, women.

Sexual harassment can take the form of a power display, intimidation or abuse from a supervisor or co-workers. It is a means of control to which women are more vulnerable because of their age or employment status. The continued segregation of women in low-paid, low-status and precarious jobs, while men predominate in better paid, authoritative and supervisory positions contributes to the problem. Some categories of women workers are especially vulnerable to sexual harassment, for example, migrants, ethnic minorities or workers in export processing zones.

Sexual harassment violates human dignity and undermines the worker's self-esteem. It affects the well-being of the worker and undermines her/his right to equal opportunity. When ignored, it can exact a high cost to an enterprise in terms of loss of productivity, workers' low morale, absenteeism, disruptions of work and staff turnover. It may also tarnish a firm's public image and decrease profits because of litigation costs.

Source: ILO: *International Women's Day, 8 March 1999, A world free of violence against women: Violence against women in the world of work* (Geneva, ILO, 1999); N. Haspels, Z.M. Kasim, C. Thomas and D. McCann: *Action against sexual harassment at work in Asia and the Pacific* (Bangkok, ILO, 2001).

---

it racial, sexual, religious or other, irrespective of their skills and work experience.[14]

Indirect discrimination

57. Indirect discrimination may occur when apparently neutral rules and practices have negative effects on a disproportionate number of members of a particular group irrespective of whether or not they meet the requirements of the job. The notion of indirect discrimination is particularly useful for policy-making. It shows that the application of the same condition, treatment or requirement to everyone can, in fact, lead to very unequal results, depending on the life circumstances and personal characteristics of the people concerned.[15] The requirement of knowledge of a particular language to obtain a job, when language competence is not indispensable, is a form of indirect discrimination based on national or ethnic origin. For example, since Latvian was recognized as the only state language in **Latvia**, shortly after independence in 1992, competence in this language has become a prerequisite for obtaining or keeping a job in all state institutions and enterprises, as well as for unemployment registration and benefits. This requirement has considerably restricted the employment opportunities available to the large number of ethnic Russians in the country.[16]

---

[14] M. Noon and E. Ogbonna (eds.): *Equality, diversity and disadvantage in employment. Introduction: The key analytical themes* (Basingstoke, Palgrove, 2001), pp. 1-14.

[15] S. Fredman: "Equality and employment issues after the incorporation of the European Convention on Human Rights", in F. Butler (ed.): *Human rights for the new millennium* (The Hague, Kluwer Law International, 2000), pp. 107-131.

[16] The number of ethnic Russians employed in certain sectors is so large, however, that dismissals would result in paralysis of the relevant services. For example, ethnic Latvians represented only 14 per cent of the police in Riga. See R.J. Dobson and G. Jones: "Ethnic discrimination: Public policy and the Latvian labour market", in *International Journal of Manpower* (Bradford, MCB University Press), Vol. 19, No. 1/2, 1998, pp. 31-47.

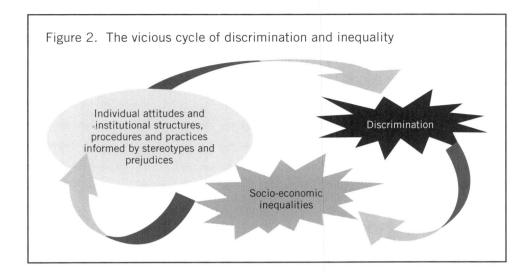

Figure 2. The vicious cycle of discrimination and inequality

Individual attitudes and institutional structures, procedures and practices informed by stereotypes and prejudices

Discrimination

Socio-economic inequalities

58. Indirect discrimination may also occur when differential treatment is accorded to particular categories of workers. Less favourable treatment of part-time workers relative to full-time workers is an example of indirect discrimination against women, who constitute the majority of part-time workers. The exclusion by law, in most countries, of domestic workers, agricultural workers or seasonal workers from social protection measures can result in indirect discrimination against various groups. Low-income women, workers belonging to ethnic minorities, migrants and elderly workers are disproportionately represented in these types of work and therefore suffer the most from this type of discrimination.

59. The notion of indirect discrimination exposes biases inherent in a wide range of institutions, rules and practices prevalent in the workplace. Work premises have traditionally been built for workers with no physical disabilities, as the standard employee. Workplace schedules, including working meetings, are often fixed according to a male model that ignores the child-rearing responsibilities of employees. These practices may effectively rule out the participation of workers who have to leave work at a fixed time to collect their children from the crèche. Such behaviour may then be interpreted as a sign of limited commitment to work and as lack of ambition.

Exposing inherent biases

60. The advantage of identifying the existence of indirect discrimination and recognizing it legally is that it permits a critical re-examination of the established practices and rules that produce different results for different groups. However, it is not always easy to determine whether and when a specific distinction between people amounts to indirect discrimination. The task is relatively simple when practices or rules that have the effect of excluding people of a particular religious belief or of a certain age from the workplace are involved. It is more complex when practices or laws have unequal effects on groups, but do not result in the total exclusion of any particular group from the workplace.

What does not constitute discrimination

61. Not all distinctions are to be considered discriminatory. Differential treatment based on the inherent requirements of a job is a perfectly legitimate practice. Therefore, where equality of opportunity is not impaired, differences in treatment do not constitute discrimination. Common examples concern the performing arts or tasks involving particular physical intimacy. Political opinion or religious belief may in certain limited circumstances constitute a

Not all distinctions are discriminatory

bona fide qualification for certain positions. For example, political affiliation may be considered in the filling of senior posts that entail special responsibilities for the development of government policy; practising a particular faith is often viewed as essential to teach in religious educational establishments.[17] The exclusion of individuals suspected of activities prejudicial to state security is not deemed to be discrimination. However, exclusions of this type must be properly and consistently defined with the requirements of the job and accompanied by procedural review protection.

The concept of merit

62. Distinctions based on individual merit do not count as discrimination in employment and occupation. The concept of merit or ability refers to a relationship between a person's talents, knowledge and skills and those required for performance of a particular job. Merit permits the best person for the job to be identified. In practice, however, merit is difficult to define and measure, and its determination is prone to bias. "Merit" is not an absolute, static concept, and the notion of what defines a "best-qualified" applicant is often determined by social values, including prejudices. Moreover, the value of different experiences and different work histories is not usually adequately measured and compared.

63. No discrimination is involved when special measures are adopted with the aim of ensuring equality of treatment and opportunity in practice for individuals with particular requirements or for groups that are disadvantaged as a consequence of past or current discrimination in the labour market. Special measures can be divided into two broad categories: special measures of protection or assistance and affirmative action measures.[18]

Special measures of protection or assistance

64. The supply of special computer software to enable employees with sight impairment to use computers or the provision of second-language classes in the workplace for recently immigrated workers are examples of special measures of assistance. Conversely, laws prohibiting women from engaging in underground work or night work fall under special measures of protection. With the shift towards the promotion of equality for women in the labour market, it is widely agreed that the protection of women at work must be pursued in the broader context of improving the living and working conditions of all workers, regardless of sex, and the promotion of equal opportunities.[19]

Pregnancy and maternity protection

65. Pregnancy and maternity protection, in the form of safeguards against dismissal or paid leave before and after confinement, transcend the sphere of protective legislation. Maternity is a condition that requires differential treatment to ensure genuine equality between men and women in the world of work. Such treatment is necessary, in particular in view of the fact that the benefits of maternity protection naturally go beyond women workers and work, and extend to society at large.

Affirmative action measures

66. Affirmative or positive action measures that aim to redress, through temporary policies, the problems of economic disadvantage or social exclusion faced by certain groups, such as women or racial and ethnic minorities, which arise out of past and present societal discrimination, will be discussed in Part II, Chapter 2.

---

[17] ILO: *Labour legislation guidelines* (Geneva, 2001).

[18] ILO: *Equality in employment and occupation*, Report III(4B), International Labour Conference, 75th Session, Geneva, 1988, paras. 139-156 and 166-169.

[19] ILO: *Night work of women in industry*, Report III(1B), International Labour Conference, 89th Session, Geneva, 2001.

Why does discrimination persist?

67. According to neoclassical economists, discrimination at work should be short-lived because it is costly and inefficient. Employers who discriminate against certain groups should disappear because they cannot compete with employers who do not discriminate. Statistical discrimination or "employers' taste" is what explains, in the view of mainstream economists, the persistence of discrimination in the labour market. The theory of statistical discrimination is based on the premise that firms cannot scrutinize the productivity of individual workers. As a consequence, they tend to rely on easily observable characteristics, such as race or sex, as an indicator of likely productivity – often assuming members of certain groups to have lower than average productivity.

68. "Employers' taste" discrimination occurs when employers prefer not to hire an individual with certain personal attributes because of fear of disruption. For example, employers may give preference in recruitment to people belonging to the same ethnic or kin group. The allocation of jobs along ethnic lines in the public sector was common practice in **Uganda** and **Kenya**, and was addressed through affirmative action programmes in the 1980s.[20]

69. Similarly, employers may decide not to hire individuals belonging to a certain religion because they are wary of prevailing negative attitudes among employees or clients towards members of this group.[21] Employers may circumvent possible hostility from their customers by assigning members of a racial or religious minority to jobs that do not entail interaction with the public. The reason given to justify this decision may be the lack of social competence to deal with the culturally dominant group.[22]

Statistical discrimination or "employers' taste"

The role of labour market institutions and processes

70. The actors within the labour market operate according to rules and norms that have been taking shape over a long period and do not necessarily adjust immediately to new patterns of behaviour. For instance, pay structures and wage-determination systems may continue to reflect traditional patterns of gender relations in the labour market, even though traditional household arrangements and gender roles and relations have been challenged. Conversely, in societies where the image of men as the breadwinners and women as secondary earners is less common, or where the wage system is more egalitarian, the gender pay gap is likely to be lower.

71. Labour market segmentation also perpetuates discrimination at work. It has the effect of excluding members of certain groups from the segments of the market characterized by greater prestige and better working conditions. The systematic confinement of certain social groups to the lower end of the labour market contributes to their economic disadvantage and low social status, and to the transmission of poverty from one generation to the next. The endurance of labour markets segmented along gender, ethnic, age or social lines in many countries challenges the prediction of mainstream economists that discrimination will

Labour market segmentation

---

[20] J. Klugman, B. Neyapti and F. Stewart: *Conflict and growth in Africa. Vol. 2: Kenya, Tanzania and Uganda* (Paris, OECD, 1999).

[21] J. Wrench: *Observations from European comparative research on discrimination in employment*, Discussion paper prepared for the RAXEN2 NFP Working Group (Vienna, European Monitoring Centre on Racism and Xenophobia, Nov. 2001).

[22] W. Knocke: "Integration or segregation? Immigrant populations facing the labour market in Sweden", in *Economic and Industrial Democracy* (London, Sage Publications), Vol. 21, No. 3, pp. 361-380.

decrease progressively, as a result of free market forces and equalization in the education and training levels across groups.

Social regulation

72. In the informal economy, where the reach of the State and formal labour market institutions is weak, differences in economic participation and returns from work are explained, to a large extent, through social regulation. This consists of unwritten values, norms and practices that shape kinship and community patterns of exchange and reciprocity, affect the roles and perceptions of particular social groups in the labour market and influence the way labour is supplied and exchanged. These values, norms and practices, often informed by ethnic, religious or caste affiliation, can strengthen commitment to work and engender a distinct culture of work. In other cases, social regulation may support a division of labour that confines certain groups to low-status and low-pay occupations, thus restricting benefits to a particular elite, and perpetuating discrimination in the process.[23]

Gatekeepers to employment and occupation

73. Access to job opportunities is controlled by "gatekeepers" to employment and occupation. These comprise a wide spectrum of actors ranging from private recruitment agencies, private or public counselling or placement services and vocational guidance institutions to private contractors and line managers. These intermediate agents can play a critical role in ensuring fairness or in perpetuating inequality and discrimination in the labour market. For example, assumptions about the unwillingness of certain businesses to hire older workers or workers with family responsibilities may lead recruitment agencies not to offer job applicants with these characteristics.[24] Moreover, asking job applicants about their place of residence is a screening device that may exclude certain individuals on the basis of their class or race. Questions on the place of residence may be used as a means to identify persons from impoverished or ethnic communities and thereby exclude them.

Denying or downplaying discrimination

74. Denial of the existence of discrimination, or its underestimation, is often at the heart of the perpetuation of unfair practices in the labour market. Denial is usually rooted in a misconception, which does not recognize the structural nature of discrimination. For example, in the case of immigrants and members of ethnic minorities in Europe, a frequent claim is that discrimination against them, caused by racism and xenophobia, acquires violent forms in society at large, but does not affect the workplace.[25]

75. Downplaying the seriousness of the problem is another, perhaps more insidious, way of hampering action against discrimination in employment and occupation. In **Brazil**, portrayed for decades as a country with exemplary achievement in racial democracy, racial prejudice and discrimination in the labour market were explained as a deplorable inheritance of the past. Class prejudice rather than race, was considered to be the main cause of the economic disadvantage and social exclusion of black people in the country. These practices were expected to vanish progressively as a result of modernization and the development of market forces. Only recently has there been recogni-

---

[23] This helps to explain why informal labour markets are as segmented as formal labour markets, and challenges conventional beliefs about the lack of barriers to entry to the informal economy. See G. Rodgers: "The creation of employment in segmented labour markets: A general problem and its implications in India", in L.K. Deshpande and G. Rodgers (eds.): *The Indian labour market and economic structural change* (Delhi, B.R. Publishing Corporation, 1994), pp. 109-139.

[24] L. Bennington: "Age and carer discrimination in the recruitment process: Has the Australian legislation failed?", in M. Noon and E. Ogbonna (eds.), op. cit., pp. 65-79.

[25] J. Wrench, op. cit.

tion that discrimination on the basis of race and colour is an issue that needs to be specifically dealt with (see Part III, Chapter 1).

76. The attitude of the victims of discrimination can perpetuate unfair practices at work. Victims of discrimination often do not challenge these practices. They may not even recognize that they are being subject to discrimination or may be unaware of their rights to equal treatment and equal opportunities and do not use these rights to redress discriminatory behaviour. Where such procedures exist, victims may decide not to make use of them because of fear of reprisals. Silence on the part of the victim may also be due to a concern that grievance procedures and judicial mechanisms may turn out to focus on "what the victim did to deserve it", rather than on what actually happened. The costliness and cumbersomeness of the judiciary or other redress systems are further disincentives. Self-restraint and self-censorship by victims of discrimination are often associated with the loss of self-esteem and self-dignity stemming from the internalization of stigma and prejudices.[26]

Self-restraint and self-censorship by victims

Why it is important to eliminate discrimination at work

77. The elimination of discrimination in the workplace is strategic to combating discrimination elsewhere. By bringing together and treating equally people with different characteristics, the workplace can help dispel prejudices and stereotypes. It can provide role models for members of disadvantaged groups to consider. Socially inclusive workplaces can pave the way for more egalitarian, democratic and cohesive labour markets and societies.

Socially inclusive workplaces

78. Equality in employment and occupation is important for the freedom, dignity and well-being of individuals. Stress, low morale and lack of motivation are prevalent sentiments among those subject to discrimination. This not only undermines their self-esteem and reinforces prejudices against them, it also affects their productivity – and, by association, the productivity of the workplace as a whole. Workers who are treated fairly and supportively work with greater commitment and goodwill for the organization. The day-to-day work atmosphere and labour relations generally improve when employees feel valued. Staff turnover, absenteeism and sick leave rates are likely to be lower, with significant cost savings for employers.

79. It has been observed that workers with disabilities, who are commonly perceived as more costly, take fewer days off for reasons other than their disability and tend to work for the same employer for longer than other employees do. An additional reason for retaining workers with disabilities is to counter the loss in firm-specific skills and experience that their dismissal would entail. The majority of these workers, in fact, tend to acquire a disability during their working life. Savings on expenditure associated with recruitment, induction and training of new staff and costs linked to absence, such as disruption of work programmes and lost output, are realized.[27] Adaptability to change

---

[26] The ingrained conviction of an insurmountable mismatch between effort and talents and actual rewards at work breeds a feeling of self-defeat and powerlessness that translates into underachievement. See G.C. Loury: *Social exclusion and ethnic groups: The challenge to economics*, Paper prepared for the Annual World Bank Conference on Development and Economics (Washington, DC, 28-30 Apr. 1999).

[27] S. Holtermann: "The costs and benefits to British employers of measures to promote equality of opportunity", in J. Humphries and J. Rubery (eds.): *The economics of equal opportunities* (Manchester, Equal Opportunities Commission, 1995), pp. 137-154.

appears to be higher when equal employment opportunities act in combination with policies aimed at raising workers' participation in decision-making.[28] Organizational commitment to equality seems to improve recruitment practices of enterprises. Studies in the **United States** have shown that affirmative action employers have more efficient recruitment and screening systems than other employers.[29]

Diversity of employees

80. The elimination of discrimination is important for the efficient functioning of labour markets and for business competitiveness. A pool of employees that does not represent the diversity of society in terms of age, sex, religion or abilities/disabilities is less likely to satisfy the needs of a customer base that is becoming increasingly heterogeneous as a result of the globalization of markets and production. For example, the relevance of broader language skills among the workers led the Public Telecommunications Service in **Sweden** to adopt a plan for ethnic equality, which encourages competencies in different languages.[30]

81. The elimination of discrimination in the labour market allows human potential to expand and to be deployed more effectively. A rise in the proportion of workers with decent work will widen the market for consumer goods and enlarge development options. Evidence shows that constraints on the employment of women translate into higher labour costs through the contraction of labour supply. Conversely, greater equality in the distribution of productive resources and in education between men and women leads to higher productivity and growth.[31]

Social fragmentation compromises economic growth

82. Systemic exclusion of members of certain groups from decent work generates serious problems of poverty and social fragmentation that compromise economic growth. The case of apartheid in **South Africa** illustrates this. Discrimination against blacks allowed whites to benefit only for a limited period of time. Eventually, apartheid became a cost to the economy. Shortages in supply of skilled labour to the manufacturing sector acted as a brake to further expansion of the economy. As the education system made it impossible for the majority of the population to compete for higher level positions, it compounded the skills blockage and contributed to further economic degradation.

83. There will always be workers who will find a job more easily than others, earn more than others or move up the occupational ladder faster than others. Differences in productivity between occupations or workers that reflect differences in skills, qualifications or abilities lead to different returns at work. This is fair and efficient. The elimination of discrimination through the promotion of equality of treatment and opportunities is not about nullifying all differences in the labour market. The goal of these policies is to make sure that differences in labour market outcomes reflect a free choice in the selection of occupations, an absence of bias in the way merit is defined and valued and equal opportunities in the acquisition and maintenance of market-relevant skills.

---

[28] V. Pérotin and A. Robinson: "Employee participation and equal opportunities practices: Productivity effect and potential complementarities", in *British Journal of Industrial Relations* (Oxford, Blackwell Publishers Ltd.), Vol. 38, No. 4, Dec. 2000, pp. 557-583.

[29] H. Holzer and D. Neumark: "Assessing affirmative action", in *Journal of Economic Literature* (Nashville, TN, American Economic Association), Vol. 38, No. 3, pp. 483-568.

[30] See A. Blackett and C. Sheppard: *Collective bargaining and equality: Theorizing the links between fundamental principles and rights at work* (Geneva, ILO Working Paper 9, 2002), p. 48.

[31] World Bank: *World Bank Policy Research Report 2001. Engendering development: Through gender equality in rights, resources and voice* (New York, Oxford University Press).

The link between discrimination and poverty

84. Discrimination in employment and occupation often exacerbates or perpetuates poverty, while poverty furthers discrimination at work in a vicious cycle. Lack of work and work that is unproductive, insecure and unprotected are the main causes of the material deprivation and vulnerability that poor people experience. Discrimination in the labour market, by excluding members of certain groups from work or by impairing their chances of developing market-relevant capabilities, lowers the quality of jobs they can aspire to. This, in turn, enhances their risk of becoming or remaining poor, which further reduces their ability to obtain jobs that can lift them out of poverty.

Discrimination exacerbates poverty

85. In **Nepal**, the Dalits, constituting some 20 per cent of the total population, are over-represented among the country's poor. As many as 80 per cent of them live below the poverty line and their share in total cultivable land is only one per cent. Unequal distribution of resources along caste lines, restrictions on free choice of occupation and exploitative relations of production are at the heart of this situation of deprivation.[32]

86. In **Australia**, the high concentration of unemployment in many aboriginal families, lower educational attainments and biased local demand explain the high proportion of discouraged workers among the indigenous youth.[33]

87. Child labour is generally associated with the poverty of parents who face discrimination in the labour market by virtue of their social or ethnic origin. Poor single-parent families, usually headed by women, and migrant families are also often forced to resort to having their children work.[34] The recent rise in labour trafficking, which disproportionately affects women and children, is related in part to sex-based discrimination in the labour market that causes unequal access for women to remunerative employment as well as to traditional beliefs that devalue girls.[35]

Discrimination and child labour

88. Cultural norms and societal beliefs on gender roles and relations are known to play a role in determining how much, and what type of education women and men acquire. In most societies, women rather than men are expected to take time off from work to look after the children or other family dependants and to undertake domestic tasks. This occurs despite abundant evidence that, in many countries, the contribution of women's paid work to the household budget is as significant as that of men and is key to keeping many households above the poverty line. The growth in single-parent families headed by women in many parts of the world confirms the importance of remunerated work for the well-being of women and for that of their children. The persistent belief that women have less need to earn an income than men may lead parents, especially in situations of scarce resources, to invest more in education for boys than for girls. This subsequently affects the quality and type of jobs women may be offered. Women's poorer economic outcomes reinforce, in turn, prevailing prejudices about what women are best suited for, e.g. lesser-skilled and, therefore, lesser-paid jobs. This leads to the systematic

Cultural norms and societal beliefs

---

[32] TEAM Consult, Pulchok, Lalitpur and Kathmandu: *Study report on discrimination and forced labour of occupational castes in Nepal*, Paper prepared for ILO Nepal (2002).

[33] B.H. Hunter and M.C. Gray: *Further investigations into indigenous labour supply: What discourages discouraged workers?*, Centre for Aboriginal Economic Policy Research, Working Paper 2/1999, pp. 18-19.

[34] ILO: *Combating the most intolerable forms of child labour: A global challenge*, Background paper prepared for the Amsterdam Child Labour Conference (Geneva, 1997), pp. 10-11.

[35] ILO: *Stopping forced labour*, Report of the Director-General, International Labour Conference, 89th Session, Geneva, 2001, para. 168.

under-valuation of their economic contribution, acts as a powerful disincentive for upgrading their skills and competencies and perpetuates their poverty.

89. Education and skill endowments are important means of overcoming disadvantaged labour market positions emanating from discrimination. People display different abilities in acquiring and developing competencies and attitudes at work that are valued by the market. This varying ability is certainly linked to individual talent and effort. But family, community background, group membership and public policy also shape people's expectations, opportunities and choices of education and work paths.[36] For example, in Latin America, illiteracy and poverty are pervasive and severe among indigenous peoples,[37] which is due also to the fact that the regions where they live are those that receive the least investment in schooling and other social and economic infrastructure, largely because indigenous people live there.[38] Underfunding, coupled with the low quality and inadequacy of the schooling received, leads to high drop-out rates, lower returns for education and, ultimately, lower earnings.

Inequality in entitlements and rights

90. Inequality in entitlements and rights – whether economic, civil or family – are another powerful source of discrimination and social exclusion. In several countries of North Africa and the Middle East, the unequal legal status of women regarding marriage and inheritance may constitute a serious disincentive to women's economic participation.[39] In **Yemen**, for instance, women need to obtain their husband's permission to work outside the home or to travel, which automatically prevents them from engaging in a number of professions. Discrimination against women in respect of inheritance also curtails women's ability to engage in gainful activities. Unequal treatment on the basis of sex in respect of nationality penalizes not only women married to non-national men but also their offspring. Education and employment opportunities, even for male family members, are considerably narrowed. To remedy this, the Council for Higher Education of **Jordan**, in 1996, further to a recommendation of the Jordanian National Commission for Women,[40] passed a decision that grants the children of Jordanian women married to non-nationals, but holding a Jordanian family civil status book, the same treatment as nationals in respect to their right to enrol at university.

---

[36] G.C. Loury: *Social exclusion and ethnic groups*, op. cit.

[37] H.A. Patrinos: *The costs of discrimination in Latin America*, Human Capital Development and Operations Policy Working Paper (Washington, DC, World Bank, 1999).

[38] A. Bello and M. Rangel: *Etnicidad, raza y equidad en América Latina y el Caribe* [Ethnicity, race and equity in Latin America and the Caribbean] (Economic Commission for Latin America and the Caribbean, 2000), p. 15.

[39] N. Hijab: *Laws, regulations, and practices impeding women's economic participation in the MENA region*, Report submitted to the World Bank, 30 Apr. 2001.

[40] The Jordanian National Commission for Women suggested to amend the Nationality Code so as to give the Council of Ministers the power to grant Jordanian nationality to the children of Jordanian women married to non-nationals who, due to their nationality, were experiencing difficulties in access to education and employment. See N. Hijab, op. cit.

3. The changing face of discrimination at work

91. Unfavourable distinctions based on sex, race or religion were among the first to be condemned and prohibited by the international community. Since then, the prevalence and seriousness of discrimination based on these features, and the forms discrimination takes, have changed. Meanwhile, labour market practices that were once considered perfectly acceptable have been declared unlawful in some countries, while others may not, or not yet, consider such practices inappropriate. With regard to sexual orientation, for example, progress has been considerable in terms of naming this as a basis for discrimination and combating it in countries such as **Australia**, **Canada**, **Netherlands**, **Slovenia**, **Sweden** and the **United States**. However, resistance even to recognition of the existence of the problem still remains fierce in most parts of the world. This chapter will briefly review the continuity, through new expressions, of old forms of discrimination, as well as identify newly recognized forms of discrimination in the world of work.

Racial discrimination: Continuity and change

92. It is not the characteristics of a person, but other people's perceptions of his or her cultural, social or physical difference, such as colour, that lead to racial discrimination.[41] In the world of work, "racial discrimination" is used to refer to arbitrary barriers to the advancement of members of linguistic communities or minorities whose identity is based on religious or cultural characteristics or even national origin. Ethnic minorities, indigenous and tribal peoples, "coloured" people and migrant workers are common victims of racial discrimination in employment and occupation. Images of their being "inferior" and "distasteful" legitimize discrimination against them.

Common victims of racial discrimination

93. Those who suffer racial discrimination are not always economically disadvantaged. People of Indian descent in East Africa and **Fiji**, people of Chinese descent in **Indonesia** or people of Indian or Chinese descent in

Racial discrimination and unemployment rates

---

[41] UNESCO has contributed to unveiling the scientific fallacies surrounding the concept of race since the 1950s. See K.J. Partsch: "Fundamental principles of human rights: Self-determination, equality and non-discrimination", in K. Vasak (ed.): *The international dimensions of human rights* (Paris, UNESCO, 1982), pp. 76-77.

Malaysia illustrate this. Very often, however, victims of racial discrimination are poor, and sometimes profoundly so. For example, in the **United States**, nearly 150 years after the end of slavery, substantial differences still exist between blacks and whites in unemployment, wages, health and mortality, as well as in incarceration rates. Although a middle class of African Americans has emerged, they still comprise a disproportionate part of the American underclass. The same holds true for those of African descent in **Brazil**.

94. Everywhere in Europe, the Roma people exhibit the highest unemployment rates compared to the rest of the population. In the **Czech Republic**, their unemployment rate averages 70 per cent, but may reach up to 90 per cent in some areas.[42] In **Romania**, between 80 and 90 per cent of the working age Roma population do not have a job.[43] The disappearance of their traditional jobs during the post-war industrial development period and declines in blue-collar worker employment after 1989 explain in part this state of affairs. Nevertheless, systemic and prolonged discrimination is expressed through substantial inequalities in education and access to, and treatment by, public agencies and institutions, including the criminal justice system.

95. Throughout South-East Asia, ethnic minorities and indigenous peoples are at a disadvantage relative to other sectors of national populations. The limited statistical evidence available suggests that they have benefited less from recent declines in poverty. In **Viet Nam**, where progress has been impressive in the past decade, the poverty rate in the country as a whole decreased from 58 to 37 per cent between 1993 and 1998. However, poverty reduction efforts have largely bypassed ethnic minorities, as the poverty rate of the regions where they are concentrated, such as the Northern and Central Highlands, remained high at 73 per cent and 91 per cent, respectively.[44]

96. In Latin America, indigenous poverty can be traced to the discrimination indigenous people face in the labour market and to the constraints in access to, and control over, land. Until recently, the participation of these people in the labour market was through various forms of coercion in agriculture and mining.[45] Today, they make up a significant proportion of temporary wage labour in commercial agriculture in countries such as **Bolivia**, **Guatemala**, and **Mexico**. While advantages can be significant in terms of daily wages compared to earnings in the communities of origin, the costs in terms of health, hygiene and lost education for their children can be severe.[46] Indigenous people's participation in urban labour markets, through informal employment, has become increasingly important as a consequence of violence, natural disasters and the impoverishment of rural areas.

"Development with identity" approach

97. The disadvantaged economic and social situation of ethnic minorities is ascribed to policy failures based on presumptions and models that did not apply to the specific circumstances of ethnic minorities. This has led many analysts to advocate a shift from policies that promote social and economic assimilation to an ethnically differentiated approach to development and poverty alleviation. Such a "development with identity" approach aims to find ways to adapt market forces to ethnic values and institutions.[47]

---

[42] European Roma Rights Centre (ERRC) Fact sheet: *Roma in the Czech Republic*, updated October 1999.

[43] ERRC Fact sheet: *Roma in Romania*, updated October 1999.

[44] R. Plant: *Indigenous peoples, ethnic minorities and poverty reduction: Regional report* (Manila, Asian Development Bank, 2002), p. 32.

[45] ILO: *Stopping forced labour*, op. cit.

[46] R. Plant: *Issues in indigenous poverty and development* (Washington, DC, Inter-American Development Bank, 1998), p. 23.

[47] R. Plant: *Indigenous peoples*, op. cit., p. 60.

98. Patterns of racial discrimination against migrant workers, second and third generations of migrants and citizens of foreign origin have changed considerably with the intensification of global migration. Although nationality is what often leads to discrimination against non-nationals, their race, colour and perceived religion are also factors. It is the perception of these workers as foreigners that may explain discriminatory behaviour against them.

Global migration

99. Throughout the world, migrant labour today is a vital asset in many sectors, including agriculture, construction, labour-intensive manufacturing, domestic work and the sex sector. This has, in some cases, led to a competition between nationals, particularly in the marginal segments of the labour force, and migrant workers who are willing to work for lesser conditions, reinforcing sentiments of racism against the newcomers. Often, however, in European countries, migrants take jobs that the locals refuse.[48] Arguments used to justify racial discrimination against immigrants have evolved. Allegations of the disruptive effects that foreign and "incompatible" cultures may have on the integrity of national identities are used instead of the older theories of purported superiority of one racial or ethnic group over another.[49]

Foreign and "incompatible" cultures

Religious discrimination: The need for better scrutiny and understanding

100. The intensification of domestic and international migration has revealed the difficulty of reconciling social cohesion and inclusion with respect for religious and cultural diversity. Particularly in the past decade, discrimination based on religion appears to have acquired greater significance. The present urgency of countering and preventing terrorism has fuelled sentiments of mutual fear and discrimination between Muslims and non-Muslims. It is clear, however, that any strategy aimed at tackling conflicts of interest should respect religious freedom; denying the basic right to follow a religion of one's choice can destabilize societies and generate violence.

101. Problems of religious discrimination in employment and occupation often arise as a result of a lack of religious freedom or intolerance towards persons of a particular faith or a different faith, or towards those who profess no religion.[50] Examples of unfair treatment in employment on religious grounds include offensive behaviour at work by co-workers or managers towards members of religious minorities, lack of respect and ignorance of religious customs, the obligation to work on religious days/holidays, biases in recruitment practices and in promotion, and lack of respect for dress restrictions. For example, the Committee of Experts on the Application of Conventions and Recommendations (CEACR) considered discriminatory the requirement that public servants and students in **Turkey** uncover their heads while on duty or at school.[51] This provision is deemed to impact disproportionately on Muslim women, possibly impairing or precluding altogether their right to equal access to education and employment because of their religious practices.

Unfair treatment on religious grounds

---

[48] E. Reyneri: *Migrants in irregular employment in the Mediterranean countries of the European Union*, International Migration Paper No. 41 (Geneva, ILO, 2001).

[49] European Commission contribution to the World Conference against Racism, Discrimination, Xenophobia and Related Intolerance, submitted to the European Conference: *All different – all equal: From principle to practice* (Strasbourg, 2000).

[50] ILO: *Equality in employment and occupation* (1988), op. cit.

[51] ILO: *Report of the Committee of Experts on the Application of Conventions and Recommendations*, Report III(1A), International Labour Conference, 89th Session, Geneva, 2001, observation concerning Convention No. 111, p. 497, para. 3.

102. In the **Islamic Republic of Iran**, a National Committee for the Promotion of the Rights of Religious Minorities (Christians, Jews and Zoroastrians) was established recently to review the problems that these minorities face and to recommend corrective measures. However, the situation of members of the Baha'i faith, an unrecognized religious minority, continues to be a source of concern. The barriers that these people face in access to higher education and to employment in public institutions are still high.[52]

Encouraging religious tolerance in society

103. The fight against religious discrimination in employment and occupation, and concrete demonstrations that religious discrimination can be eliminated in the workplace, constitute a useful pathway to encourage religious tolerance in society. The dynamics and manifestations of religious discrimination in the workplace have not been researched as much, and as well, as other forms of discrimination. This is related in part to the difficulty of discussing a topic that is seen as pertaining to the private sphere and to the broader question of freedom of conscience. Another constraint, as in the case of national origin or political opinion, deals with the legal prohibition in many countries on requesting or gathering information about religion. In practice, detecting and distinguishing religious discrimination from discrimination based on race or national extraction is often problematic because religion, race and national extraction are closely intertwined and are often perceived as together defining distinct cultural or ethnic identities.[53]

104. Systematic and informed work on religious discrimination at work is confined to a few countries, particularly Northern Ireland[54] and, to a lesser extent, the **United States**.[55] In more recent times, however, management's interest in religious discrimination in the workplace appears to have grown, as awareness has increased of the potential related legal and economic liabilities. A similar trend is to be expected in Europe as a consequence of the adoption by the European Union of Council Directive 2000/78/EC (27 November 2000) establishing a general framework for equal treatment in employment and occupation. This Directive requests Member States to enact, within a specified time frame, legislation prohibiting, inter alia, religious discrimination in employment.

The challenge of eliminating discrimination against people living with HIV/AIDS

105. As a result of the magnitude and disruptive social, economic and political implications of the HIV/AIDS pandemic, discrimination at work based on HIV/AIDS status is an issue of growing concern across the world.

106. Approximately 42 million men, women and children worldwide are estimated to be living with HIV/AIDS. The socio-economic and sexual discrim-

---

[52] ILO: *Report of the Committee of Experts on the Application of Conventions and Recommendations*, Report III(1A), International Labour Conference, 90th Session, Geneva, 2002, observation concerning Convention No. 111, p. 493, paras. 11-12.

[53] M.F. Fernádez López and J. Calvo Gallego: *La discriminación por razones religiosas en Italia, España, Francia y los países hispanoparlantes y francófonos* [Discrimination on religious grounds in Italy, Spain, France and Spanish- and French-speaking countries], Background paper prepared for this fourth Global Report.

[54] D. Smith and G. Chambers: *Inequality in Nothern Ireland* (Oxford, Oxford University Press, 1991) and C. McCrudden: "The Northern Ireland Fair Employment White Paper: A critical assessment", in *The Industrial Law Journal* (London, Sweet and Maxwell Ltd.), Vol. 17, No. 3, September 1988, pp. 162-181.

[55] M. Lipson: *Literature review for religious discrimination in the workplace*, Background paper prepared for this fourth Global Report (Geneva, ILO, 2001).

ination experienced by women increase their vulnerability to HIV/AIDS. Rates of HIV/AIDS infection among women have been rising, and young women aged 15-24 are now twice as likely to be infected as young men of the same age group.[56]

107. In the world of work, discrimination against workers with known or suspected HIV/AIDS may originate from co-workers, customers, service suppliers and employers. Fear, ignorance and the prejudices surrounding the illness, and a lack of information about the prevention and the transmission of the virus are at the heart of discrimination at work based on HIV/AIDS status. Concerns with the costs that employing an HIV-positive worker may entail, in terms of both declines in productivity and increases in labour costs, also play an important role.

HIV/AIDS – fear, ignorance and prejudice

108. Discrimination at work against people with known or suspected HIV/AIDS can take many forms. Pre-employment testing, which results in a refusal to hire, is widespread, even where national and workplace policies against discrimination based on HIV/AIDS are in place, including in southern Africa. A growing number of countries require mandatory HIV/AIDS testing from long-term foreign visitors (i.e. students and workers) prior to entry.[57] In some Asian countries, migrant women workers are subjected to compulsory HIV/AIDS tests.[58]

109. Breach of medical confidentiality is also frequent and this, in turn, leads to either dismissal or resignation. The pressures and hostility towards HIV-positive workers are sometimes such that they feel compelled to resign even though they have not been formally dismissed. An ILO study found breach of confidentiality and dismissal to be widespread in **Brazil**, **Côte d'Ivoire**, **France**, **Hungary**, **India**, **Indonesia**, **Jamaica**, **Mexico**, **South Africa**, **Thailand**, **Uganda** and the **United States**.[59] Other forms of discrimination may be dismissal without medical evidence, notice or a hearing, demotion to positions of lower experience and skill, denial of insurance benefits to pay for AIDS-related expenses, reduction in salary, or harassment.[60]

Hostility towards HIV-positive workers

110. Discrimination is severe against workers who perform economic activities subject to social disapproval or considered to be illegal, such as sex workers or migrant workers. HIV/AIDS also reinforces patterns of gender inequality through its effects on the female members of families affected by the epidemic. The burden of caring for HIV-infected family and community members falls more often on women and girls, thereby increasing their workload and diminishing their income-generating and schooling possibilities. Older women workers may have to assume responsibility for orphaned grandchildren, although their skills are not granted any economic value.

---

[56] UNAIDS: *AIDS epidemic update December 2002* (Geneva, UNAIDS, 2002).

[57] In February 2002, the United States Department of State listed 60 countries requiring such testing. See http://travel.state.gov/HIVtestingreqs.html

[58] United Nations: *Report of the Asian-Pacific regional seminar of experts on migrants and trafficking in persons with particular reference to women and children: Note by the Secretary-General*, World Conference against Racism, Racial Discrimination, Xenophobia and Related Intolerance, Geneva, 21 May-1 June 2001, doc. A/CONF.189/PC.2/3, para. 49.

[59] L. N'Daba and J. Hodges-Aeberhard: *HIV/AIDS and employment* (Geneva, ILO, 1998), pp. 3 and 31-34.

[60] T. de Bruyn: *HIV/AIDS and discrimination: A discussion paper* (Montreal, Canadian HIV/AIDS Legal Network and Canadian AIDS Society, 1998).

Discrimination on the grounds of disability

111. According to World Health Organization (WHO) estimates, between 7 and 10 per cent of the world's population live with disabilities, and this proportion is likely to grow in the future with the ageing of the population. The vast majority lives in developing countries, and rural disability rates appear to be higher than urban rates. Disability rates for women seem to be higher than those for men in developed countries, and lower than those for men in developing countries. Conversely, it seems that severe impairment may be a male-dominated issue. Disability also has very strong ethnic connotations. In the **United States**, in the 18-69 working-age group, Native Americans display the highest percentage of limitation in work, due to chronic conditions (17.3 per cent).[61] In both developed and developing countries, disabled people have lower education and income levels and are less likely to have savings than the rest of the population. Disability adds to the risk of poverty, and conditions of poverty increase the risk of disability.

112. Wars and military conflicts are important causes of disability, particularly psychological disabilities that often remain undiagnosed and unrecorded. Refugees from conflicts are also vulnerable to potentially disabling illnesses because of the conditions they endure during their journeys and in camps.

Disability – a broad and fluid category

113. The term "disability" does not mean merely a medical condition; rather, it constitutes a broad and fluid category, associated with social disadvantages and restrictions. People with disabilities face stigmatization and limited understanding of their abilities and aspirations. People can move into a state of disability at different stages in their lives, at birth or later in life, and during further education or while in employment. Disabilities can be acquired in diverse ways, may take different forms and may constitute physical, sensory, intellectual or mental impairment. Because of their heterogeneity, disabilities can affect differently the ability of the people concerned to work and they require different types of accommodation measures. This, in turn, gives rise to diverse forms of discrimination.

114. The most common form of discrimination is the denial of opportunities to the disabled either to work altogether or to build on their abilities and potential. The unemployment rates of persons with disabilities reach an estimated 80 per cent or more in many developing countries. In Eastern Europe, unemployment rates for the disabled and the region's share of the total number of unemployed jobseekers rose sharply in the 1990s due to recession and restructuring of the economic system.

115. The majority of disabled persons tends to be concentrated in occupations and industries with low entry barriers or in reserved jobs. In **Brazil** and **Costa Rica**, the chances of disabled persons being offered a job in the formal market are scarce, the most common option being instead to work in small, informal family units in agriculture and services. This explains, in part, the differences in average wages of disabled and non-disabled people: non-disabled workers earn 45.8 per cent more than disabled workers in **Brazil** and 11.5 per cent more in **Costa Rica**, where the definition of disability is wider.[62]

---

[61] United States National Institute on Disability and Rehabilitation Research: *Chartbook on work and disability in the United States, 1998* (Washington, DC), p. 28. See also at www. infouse.com/disabilitydata/workdisability_3_5.html

[62] G. Hernández Licona: "Disability and the labour market in Latin America", Paper submitted to the annual conference of the Inter-American Development Bank, Chile, March 2001, in *Disability World*, Issue No. 9, July-August 2001 at http://www.disabilityworld.org/07-08_01/labour1.shtml

116. People with disabilities are often given low-paid, unskilled and menial tasks or belong to the "last hired – first fired" group of workers who are more vulnerable to the effects of recession. To a significant extent, higher unemployment among disabled persons is a result of discrimination in education and training. The educational system is often not organized to meet the needs of disabled persons, and training offered in specialized centres often provides a narrow range of skills. The development of information and communication technologies opens up new avenues for both education and employment. By removing physical barriers, distance learning and teleworking offer new opportunities to some categories of people with disabilities. .

Disabled people – last hired – first fired

117. Disabled people also encounter discrimination in the labour market as a result of employers' and co-workers' misconceptions about their abilities and a lack of adapted working environments. The employers who hire disabled persons have two main concerns: the costs entailed in hiring persons with disabilities may be higher if they need special facilities or if adjustments to the physical environment are required; and the productivity of disabled persons may be affected by the impairments from which they suffer. This seems to be a particular concern for employers in small businesses. A study carried out in the **United Kingdom**, showed that among employers with disabled employees more than half did not have to make any adjustments to the physical environment; and when these were made, most changes had not been costly or difficult to make.[63]

Age as a determinant of discrimination in the labour market

118. The importance of tackling discrimination based on age is evident when considering the shift in the age structure of the world population. The pace of ageing is different between countries and regions. Developing countries still have relatively young populations while industrialized countries have relatively old populations. But developing-country populations are ageing faster than those in industrialized countries. It has been projected that by 2050, 33 per cent of people in developed countries and 19 per cent in developing countries will be 60 or older, and the latter will amount to 1.6 billion persons, i.e. over 80 per cent of the world's elderly population.[64] The majority of older persons worldwide are women, constituting 55 per cent of the over-60 age group, and 61 per cent of the over-80 age group.[65] This feminization of later life is more marked in developed countries, although the gap between female and male life expectancy is widening at a faster rate in developing countries.

Shift in age structure

119. "Oldness" is a relative concept and its perception changes over time and across cultures. Statutory retirement age varies between countries. Within the same country, it may differ according to the branch of activity, and, within the same industry, it may differ according to sex. Everywhere, however, older workers face discrimination, although the reasons vary.

120. In many developing countries, increasing export dependency, international indebtedness and industrialization have drawn resources away from

---

[63] Institute of Employment Studies and MORI: *Impact on small business of lowering the Disability Discrimination Act Part II threshold* (Stratford-on-Avon, Disability Rights Commission, 2001).

[64] United Nations: *World Population Prospects: The 2000 revision: Highlights*, Draft doc. ESA/P/WP.165, February 2001 (New York, United Nations), pp. 14-15.

[65] HelpAge International: *State of the world's older people 2002* (London, 2002), p. 4.

regions and sectors such as agricultural production and informal trade, where older people, especially women, are more active. In many of the transition economies of Eastern Europe and the former Soviet Union, high unemployment has intensified competition for jobs of all kinds, with older people increasingly marginalized from all job opportunities.[66]

Older workers face barriers to employment

121. The barriers that older workers face in finding employment are high, and once they lose their jobs they find it difficult to find new employment.[67] In OECD countries, older workers are over-represented among the long-term unemployed. Exclusion from jobs can result from overt discrimination, in the form of age limits for hiring, or may acquire more subtle forms, such as allegations of lack of "career potential" or "too much experience". Discrimination on the grounds of age is not limited to near-retirement age. A survey carried out in **Estonia** in 1998 showed that employers' perceptions of a female worker being a certain age played a significant role in decreasing the employment opportunities for women. Employers consistently discriminated against older women workers in occupations such as secretaries, salespersons and service workers, where employers preferred youthful-looking women below 30.[68]

122. Older workers are also discriminated against in the form of age limits for training. In the European Union, while almost half the workers over 50 work in firms that provide training, less than 15 per cent take part in training measures – either employer-provided or private.[69] In countries where wage increases are linked to seniority, firms might be tempted to replace older workers by less-costly younger ones.

123. Indirect discrimination might be more difficult to detect. This generally consists of measures that create the conditions that compel older workers to retire early. These measures can include offers of voluntary retirement options, accompanied by more or less subtle pressures to accept them. For instance, a survey conducted in the **United Kingdom** has revealed that, between 1991 and 1996, six out of ten organizations in the survey admitted that they targeted older workers.[70]

Multiple discrimination: The accumulation of deprivation

124. People experience discrimination in the labour market differently. The intensity or severity of the disadvantages that they may confront depends on the number and interplay of the personal characteristics that generate discrimination against them. For example, a person may be different in race/colour, e.g. black; a black person may be a woman; a woman may have a physical disability; a person with a disability may be old; and one person can have all these characteristics, e.g. be an older, disabled, black woman, and therefore experience very complex forms of discrimination.

---

[66] HelpAge International: *The ageing and development report: Poverty, independence and the world's older population* (London, 1999), p. 9.

[67] ILO: *World Employment Report 1998-99* (Geneva, 1999), pp. 188-191.

[68] ILO: *Realizing decent work for older women workers* (Geneva, 2000), p. 15.

[69] European Commission: *Report requested by Stockholm European Council: "Increasing labour force participation and promoting active ageing"*, Report from the Commission to the Council, the European Parliament, the Economic and Social Committee and the Committee of the Regions (Brussels, 2002), p. 5.

[70] Arrowsmith and McGoldrich, 1996, quoted in A. Samorodov: *Ageing and labour markets for older workers*, Employment and Training Paper No. 33 (Geneva, ILO, 1999), p. 16.

125. The disadvantages or deprivations that women experience because of gender cannot be separated from the disadvantages stemming from other personal attributes and identities related to their religion, race or national extraction. The interplay of identities results in experiences of exclusion and disadvantage that are unique to those with multiple identities. In **Brazil**, recent labour-market data disaggregated by colour and sex show that the gap in terms of employment and unemployment rates and pay between white and black women has been widening over the past years.[71] This suggests that race and class have been key determinants of the differential impact that policies directed at enhancing gender equality have had on women workers.

Interplay of identitites

126. Intersectional analysis arose from the recognition that the traditional understanding of discrimination based on specific grounds (e.g. racial discrimination) did not include experiences that were particular to specific subgroups of persons (e.g. women).[72] From there, intersectional analysis has evolved into an understanding that all grounds of discrimination may interact with each other and produce specific experiences of discrimination. This approach is particularly useful in exposing new forms of discrimination that have remained hidden from the public, directing attention to those who are most disadvantaged. Such insights into discrimination should lead to more effective policies to combat the phenomenon.

Discrimination grounds may interact

127. Discrimination has clear life-cycle dimensions. If no remedial action is taken, disadvantages tend to accumulate and intensify over time, with negative repercussions for life after work and for society more generally. Gender inequalities in social protection reveal the perverse consequences of direct and indirect forms of discrimination against women throughout working life. Women's interrupted careers, lower pay and shorter contributions, and earlier retirement records, mean that social protection benefits are, on average, lower for women than they are for men. Women are often excluded from company pension and health plans as a result of their lower status or insufficient years of service. In mandatory retirement saving schemes, women receive lower pensions than men where the pension is calculated according to the longer life expectancy of women. Gender-based unequal entitlements to income at retirement age have serious implications for social and employment policies in the light of the feminization of later life across all regions.[73] This points to the relevance of a life-cycle approach to the fight against discrimination.

Life-cycle dimension of discrimination

---

[71] A.S.A. Guimarães: "Las causas de la pobreza negra en Brasil: algunas reflexiones" ["The causes of black poverty in Brazil: Some reflections"], in *Raza y pobreza: consulta interagencias sobre Afrolatinoamericanos* [Race and poverty: Interagency consultation on Afro-Latin Americans], Latin American and Caribbean Region Sustainable Development Working Paper No. 9: Preliminary report (Inter-American Dialogue, World Bank and Inter-American Development Bank, November 2000), pp. 51-58.

[72] T. Makkonen: *Multiple, compound and intersectional discrimination: Bringing the experiences of the most marginalized to the fore* (Turku Åbo, Åbo Akademi University, Institute for Human Rights, 2002).

[73] ILO: *Gender, poverty and employment: A reader's kit* (Geneva, 2000).

Part II. Selected trends and policy issues

1. Gender inequalities in the labour market as a proxy for sex-based discrimination at work

128. As there are no labour market indicators that measure directly discrimination at work, this chapter will use four sets of data that are universally recognized as valid substitutes. These are gender disparities in respect of labour force participation rates, unemployment rates, remuneration and the jobs performed by most women and by most men.

129. While still limited and patchy, data disaggregated for sex are more readily available than data disaggregated for other types of social categorization. A brief discussion of some of this data is presented for illustrative purposes, to indicate comparable paths for analysis of discrimination with respect to other groups when data on these become available (e.g. for racial and ethnic groups, workers of different national origin, persons with disabilities, older workers).

Discrimination at entry to the labour market

130. One way of assessing discrimination at entry to the labour market is by considering the relative levels of participation in the labour force. ILO information available on women's participation in the labour market for 1990 and 2000 presents a varied picture (see Annex 3, table 1). While the female labour force participation rate continued to rise in most developed countries and in Latin America and the Caribbean, this rise was more moderate in Asian countries, where in certain cases the impact of the financial crisis appears to have hit women harder than men in terms of falling labour force participation rates. In transition economies and in sub-Saharan Africa, the rate has been declining for both women and men. In a number of cases, where the gap between male and female labour force participation rates continued to narrow, this resulted from reduced or stagnating rates for men and rising rates for women.

Relative levels of participation in the labour force

131. Discrimination raises hurdles for some groups at entry to the labour market; it also makes it harder to remain in employment. Women, and in particular those with low levels of education and those who are older, are at greater risk of losing their jobs and face more difficulties re-entering the labour force than men do.

132. Unemployment rates have almost always been higher for women than for men. In recent years, there have been notable exceptions (see Annex 3, table 2). The unemployment rate has been lower for women than for men in the Baltic States, in parts of East Asia and in developed countries such as **Australia, Canada, Japan, New Zealand** and the **United Kingdom**. This may be due to the fact that the jobs on offer have terms of employment that women accept more readily than men (e.g. precarious contracts, low-paid employment), and that employers prefer workers with certain characteristics (e.g. female workers in export processing zones). However, one has to be cautious in interpreting falling trends in unemployment rates. Women, and for that matter other discriminated-against groups, may adjust to deteriorating labour market conditions by (i) accepting shorter working hours rather than no work at all, and, therefore, becoming underemployed, and (ii) in the face of discrimination becoming discouraged and abandoning active jobseeking altogether. Underemployment and the phenomenon of "discouraged workers" are more widespread among discriminated-against groups and tend to mask higher, true unemployment rates.

133. The increased participation of women in paid employment worldwide has certainly made their economic contribution more visible, and may indicate lower levels of discrimination at entry to employment. But has women's status improved? To answer this question, it is necessary to look at the type and quality of jobs available to women, in relation to those available to men.

Employment status differs between men and women

134. The employment status of men and that of women display different features. Men are more likely to be in core or regular and better remunerated positions, whereas women are often in peripheral, insecure, less-valued positions. Recruitment practices that favour men, or barriers in the promotion or career development of women, have the effect of excluding women or "segregating" them into certain jobs. Women are heavily represented among part-time workers (see figure 3). In the 1990s, the share of part-time work to total employment rose in most of the industrialized countries but fell in several Latin American and Caribbean countries for both men and women. In **Japan** and the **United States**, almost 70 per cent of all part-time workers were women by the end of the decade. Where part-time work has been rising for women, it appears to be increasingly involuntary.[1]

135. The increase of permanent temporary employment (i.e. when workers have continuously extended short-term, fixed-term or temporary contracts, or have such contracts with short breaks in between) tends to be directed disproportionately at women workers and other discriminated-against groups, regardless of their educational level. Women are also over-represented among homeworkers, casual workers and temporary workers. In self-employment, proportionately more men than women are employers, while women are more likely to be own-account workers and in the informal economy. Finally, women overwhelmingly dominate the category of contributing (often unpaid) family workers.

136. The increase in women's employment in the non-agricultural sector is an indicator of the progress in achieving one of the Millennium Development Goals, in terms of promoting gender equality and empowering women. Here, there seems to have been an improvement in most countries (see Annex 3, table 1).

---

[1] ILO: *Key Indicators of the Labour Market (KILM) 2001-02* (Geneva, 2002), p. 721.

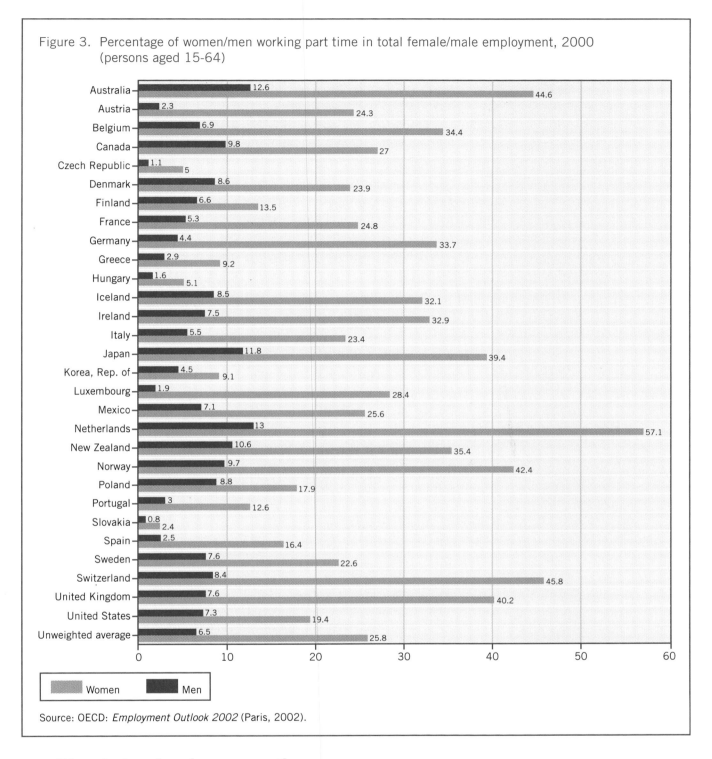

Figure 3. Percentage of women/men working part time in total female/male employment, 2000 (persons aged 15-64)

Source: OECD: *Employment Outlook 2002* (Paris, 2002).

Discrimination in occupation

137. Once an individual has overcome the hurdle of entering the labour market, she or he may continue to suffer from discriminatory treatment. For example, women may decide to abandon a certain professional path because they anticipate discrimination. One way of looking at such discrimination is through patterns of occupational segregation. This refers to the fact that men and women tend to work in different sectors of the economy and hold different positions within the same occupational group. Truck drivers, for instance, are usually men, while women tend to predominate in dressmaking or domestic

Discrimination and patterns of occupational segregation

2.

work (horizontal segregation). Within the same occupation, women make up the bulk of production workers, while men tend to predominate in production supervision (vertical segregation).

138. Occupational segregation is frequently regarded as evidence of inequality as it includes aspects of social stratification in power, skills and earnings. All are related and may be taken as indicators of social advantage or disadvantage. Occupational segregation by sex has been more detrimental to women than to men: "female" occupations are generally less attractive, with a tendency towards lower pay, lower status and fewer advancement possibilities. Similar discriminatory processes operate along the lines of race, ethnic origin, age, disability and health status, among others, and result in the undervaluation and segregation of groups of workers into jobs with less favourable terms and conditions of employment.

Determinants of occupational segregation

139. Social, cultural, historical and economic factors all play a part in determining the extent and the patterns of occupational segregation around the world. These factors include:

— social norms and stereotypical perceptions regarding men and women, family life and working life;[2]

— education and vocational training;

— taxation and social security regimes, and welfare policies and institutions;

— the structure of the labour market, including the size of the informal economy;

— discrimination at entry to the labour market and at work.

Welfare policies and institutions also impinge on women's opportunities in different spheres of life, including in the labour market (see box 1.1).

Box 1.1

State gender equality policy:
A four-model typology of industrialized countries

■ *Formal egalitarian model* (e.g. the United States), with a formal commitment to gender equality in the labour market evidenced by legislation but with limited state-sponsored services such as childcare.

■ *Substantive egalitarian model* (e.g. Nordic countries), with both a formal commitment to gender equality and the provision of substantive support services for working women.

■ *Traditional family-centred model* (e.g. Japan), with few or no formal-legal commitments and no substantive services for working women.

■ *Economy-centred model* (e.g. Hungary), with many services for working women but little or no formal commitment to gender equality.

Where support services to mothers are well developed, female labour force participation is higher and goes hand in hand with high occupational segregation, as welfare services are dominated by women workers. The traditional family-centred model might be less likely to remain viable in the long run because of the growing pervasiveness of gender egalitarian ideals.

Source: M.L. Chang: "The evolution of sex segregation regimes", in *American Journal of Sociology* (Chicago, University of Chicago Press), Vol. 105, No. 6, May 2000, pp. 1658-1701.

---

[2] P. Bourdieu: *La domination masculine* [Male domination] (Paris, Le Seuil, 1998).

Trends in occupational segregation[3]

140. The main difficulty in measuring changes in the degree of occupational segregation is to distinguish between changes in vertical and horizontal segregation. Comparisons are made more difficult by the fact that the classification of occupations dominated by women is less detailed than the classification of occupations dominated by men.

141. "Sex-dominated" occupations may be defined as those where workers of one sex constitute more than 80 per cent of the labour force. While approximately one-half of workers are in sex-dominated occupations, women are employed in a narrower range of occupations than men; male-dominated non-agricultural occupations are seven times as many as female-dominated occupations.[4]

Sex-dominated occupations

142. The level of horizontal occupational segregation by sex is lowest in the Asia-Pacific region and highest in the Middle East/North Africa. It is also relatively high in other developing countries, while of average magnitude in the OECD countries (although there are large and significant differences among OECD countries, with the **United States** displaying the lowest level of horizontal occupational segregation by sex and Scandinavian countries the highest).[5] Regional results also show that there is great variation within the Asian region, whereas for the other regions, results are more similar across countries (see Annex 3, table 3).

Horizontal occupational segregation

143. In the 1980s and the 1990s, horizontal segregation fell in a majority of countries. It dropped most in countries where it was relatively high (e.g. in several small developing countries and in a few OECD countries), and remained unchanged in countries where it was relatively low. However, the opposite trend was observed in **China** and **Hong Kong, China**, and, in the 1990s, occupational segregation also increased in the transition economies.[6] There was an increase in horizontal occupational segregation by sex in **China** in the 1980s and 1990s, as women's role and status were redefined with the economic reforms.[7] On the one hand, women have been encouraged to withdraw from traditionally male-dominated industries;[8] on the other hand, new employment opportunities have been created in export-oriented industries, such as the garment industry, where women predominate.

144. It seems that, as horizontal segregation declines, vertical segregation frequently tends to increase. Export-led industrial development has opened up many industrial occupations to women, without, however, decreasing gender inequalities within occupation in terms of pay, authority and career advancement possibilities. It is still difficult for women to break through the "glass ceiling"[9] (see table 1).

Vertical occupational segregation

145. Over time, women have been increasing their share in administrative and managerial work,[10] but the nature of their career paths tends to block

Women excluded from networks

---

[3] Figures presented here are illustrative and are based on ILO SEGREGAT data.

[4] R. Anker: *Gender and jobs: Sex segregation of occupations in the world* (Geneva, ILO, 1998).

[5] ibid.

[6] It is not clear whether the increase in occupational sex segregation in the transition countries in Europe is due to real deterioration over the past decade or to a shift toward using Western occupational classifications.

[7] Survey Report of Social Status of Women in China, Phase II, carried out by the All China Women's Federation and the National Statistics Bureau.

[8] M. Zhao: "The consequences of China's socialist market economy for seafarers", in *Work, Employment and Society* (London, Sage Publications), Vol. 16(1), 2002, pp. 171-183.

[9] L. Wirth: *Breaking through the glass ceiling: Women in management* (Geneva, ILO, 2001).

[10] United Nations Development Fund for Women: *Progress of the World's Women 2000: UNIFEM Biennial Report* (New York, UNIFEM, 2000), p. 91, chart 4.3.

Table 1.   Share of female administrators in countries with ISCO-88[a] data, 2000[b]

Region	Administrators as a percentage of the total labour force	Percentage of female administrators
Developed countries	8.1	27.6
Transition economies	6.7	32.9
Asia and the Pacific	5.6	15.3
Latin America and the Caribbean	5.0	32.8
Middle East and North Africa	5.9	28.1

Notes: [a] International Standard Classification of Occupations (ISCO-88), major, sub-major and minor groups. [b] More disaggregated data would show even greater vertical segregation (see H. Melkas and R. Anker: *Gender-based occupational segregation*, Background paper prepared for this fourth Global Report (Geneva, ILO, 2002).
Source: *ILO Yearbook of Labour Statistics*, 2001 (Geneva, 2001).

their progress to top positions. At lower management levels, women are typically placed in non-strategic sectors and in personnel and administrative positions rather than in professional and line-management jobs leading to the top. Women are seldom found in product development and corporate finance. Often these initial disadvantages are compounded by women being excluded from the networks, both formal and informal, that are so essential for advancement within enterprises. Participation in decision-making proves to be one of the most resistant areas for gender equality.

146.   Changes in the occupational structure of the labour force constitute another, less influential, factor contributing to the downward trend in occupational segregation.[11] In a majority of countries, the main source of employment for both women and men is now the service sector, where the concentration of women is higher by about 20 per cent, and is even over 30 per cent in some countries. Women dominate in retail trade and hotel and restaurant services, and especially in the community, social and personal services that are traditionally associated with their gender roles. Domestic service is almost exclusively female and there is also a higher proportion of women in health, education and social services. However, the better-paying service-sector jobs, in financial services, real estate and business services and public administration, are dominated by men.

"New" occupations –
a window of opportunity

147.   It is informative to look at women's presence in "new" occupations related to information and communication technologies. These new jobs were considered a window of opportunity for equal treatment and equal opportunities for women, since they required fewer of the traditionally recognized male attributes, physical strength, for example, than the established occupations where men have fared better than women. Two examples of new occupations are those of computer programmer and systems analyst. These are rapidly growing and well-paid professional occupations. The share of women in these occupations varies widely across countries (see table 2). However, the little evidence available shows that occupational segregation persists in these new areas of work. In the 1990s, women's share in these occupations dropped in several countries, the largest decline occurring in **Poland**, while there was a small increase of 1.9 per cent in **Hong Kong, China**.

The need for women-
supportive policies

148.   It is clear that changing the gender structure of the labour market and eliminating obstacles to free and informed individual choices has proven to be a very slow process everywhere. Some improvement has been observed in horizontal occupational sex segregation; however, patterns of vertical occupa-

---

[11] R. Anker, op. cit.

Table 2. Women in "new" occupations of computer programmer and systems analyst, 1990-2000

Country	Latest year	Percentage of women in "new" occupations (latest year)	Representation ratio[a] (latest year)	Change in percentage of women in "new" occupations, 1990-2000[b]
Belarus	1999	50.9	1.00	—
France	1999	19.6	0.43	–2.3
Germany	2000	18.0	0.42	—
Hong Kong, China	2001	23.8	0.54	1.9
Korea, Republic of	2000	23.4	0.65	—
Poland	2001	25.0	0.55	–44.1
Thailand	2000	47.7	0.98	—
United States	2000	28.5	0.60	–5.3
Average (unweighted)		29.6	0.65	–12.5

Notes: [a] The representation ratio is per cent female in an occupation divided by per cent female for the entire non-agricultural labour force. It shows the extent to which an occupation is more (when value is above 1.0) or less (when value is below 1.0) feminized than usual for the country. [b] The percentage of change is adjusted to a ten-year period (e.g. if change is measured over a five-year period, the value would be doubled; if over a 20-year period, it would be halved). Change data are available for France (1990-1999), United States (1991-2000), Poland (1994-2000) and Hong Kong, China (1991-2001). — = Figures not available.

Source: H. Melkas and R. Anker: *Gender-based occupational segregation,* Background paper prepared for this fourth Global Report (Geneva 2002), Table A.

tional sex segregation continue to be reproduced around the world. The old gender biases will persist, unless the new job opportunities are accompanied by women-supportive policies. [12]

Discrimination in remuneration

Where does the problem lie and why is it important to tackle it?

149. Addressing discrimination in remuneration entails identifying the factors that account for imbalances in pay in order to determine whether those imbalances are a result of discrimination. Discrimination in remuneration occurs when the main basis for the determination of wages is not the content of the work to be performed, but rather the sex, the colour or other personal attributes of the person performing the work. Detecting discrimination in pay is a challenging task and several approaches have been followed. One approach distinguishes between inequalities due to individual characteristics, such as levels of education, skills or seniority, and inequalities due to discrimination (see Annex 3, table 4). A second approach focuses on inequalities among groups and finds that women's pay or earnings in certain occupations, sectors, skills or levels of pension is typically lower than men's, irrespective of individual abilities. This approach argues that these inequalities can only be explained by discrimination. [13]

---

[12] ILO: *World Employment Report 2001: Life at work in the information economy* (Geneva, 2001).

[13] Various international studies have shown that around one-third of the female-male pay differential is due to occupational segregation by sex (see R. Anker, op. cit.), and that about 10-30 per cent of the gender pay gap remains "unexplained" (see K. Nurmi: *Gender and labour market in the EU* (Helsinki, Ministry of Social Affairs and Health, 1999). Differentials in women's and men's income also extend to pensions.

Achieving genuine gender equality

150. The elimination of discrimination in remuneration is crucial to achieving genuine gender equality and promoting social equity and decent work. No lasting improvements in the economic status of women and other discriminated-against groups can be expected as long as the market rewards their time at a lower rate than that of the dominant group. Convention No. 100 and its accompanying Recommendation (see box 1.2) provide policy guidance on how

---

Box 1.2

Equal Remuneration Convention, 1951 (No. 100) and its accompanying Recommendation (No. 90)

Convention No. 100 and Recommendation No. 90 list a number of measures to promote and ensure the application of "the principle of equal remuneration for men and women workers for work of equal value".

Convention No. 100 establishes that remuneration rates are to be established without discrimination based on the sex of the worker. Furthermore, it requires that men and women workers obtain equal remuneration for work of equal value and not just for the same or similar work. The implementation of this principle requires a comparison among jobs to determine their relative value. Since men and women tend to work in different occupations, it is important to have systems that can objectively measure the relative value of jobs that differ in content and skill requirements.

What is remuneration?

The term "remuneration" includes "the ordinary, basic or minimum wage or salary and any additional emoluments whatsoever payable directly or indirectly, whether in cash or in kind, by the employer to the worker and arising out of the worker's employment" (Convention No. 100, Article 1(a)).

The principle of equal remuneration may be applied by means of:

(a) national laws or regulations;

(b) legally established or recognized machinery for wage determination;

(c) collective agreements between employers and workers; or

(d) a combination of these various means (Article 2).

The application of the principle of equal remuneration:
A common responsibility of the State and the social partners

Ratifying States must ensure the application of the principle of equal remuneration in the areas where they are involved in wage fixing. When they are not directly involved, they have the obligation to promote the observance of this principle by those who are involved in the determination of remuneration rates. States must cooperate with employers' and workers' organizations to implement the Convention and must involve them in the establishment, where appropriate, of objective job evaluation methods. Employers' and workers' organizations are also responsible for the effective application of this principle.

Discrimination in the determination of remuneration rates is not the only source of pay differentials between men and women. A wide range of pre-market and labour market factors also impinge upon women's equal opportunities at work, including in pay. "In order to facilitate the application of the principle of equal remuneration for men and women workers for work of equal value", the Recommendation encourages the adoption of measures ensuring that "workers of both sexes have equal or equivalent facilities for vocational guidance or employment counselling, for vocational training and for placement", and "to encourage women to use these facilities", and "providing welfare and social services which meet the needs of women workers, particularly those with family responsibilities" (Paragraph 6). Measures promoting equality as regards access to occupations and posts are also suggested.

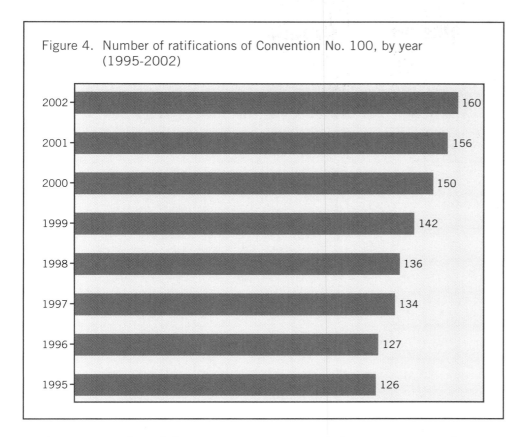

Figure 4. Number of ratifications of Convention No. 100, by year (1995-2002)

Year	Number
2002	160
2001	156
2000	150
1999	142
1998	136
1997	134
1996	127
1995	126

to eliminate sex-based discrimination in respect of remuneration and to promote the principle of equal pay for work of equal value. This Convention is among the most widely ratified ILO Conventions (see figure 4), and more ratifications are expected. According to information provided to the Office, the ratification process has been initiated in **Antigua and Barbuda** and **Kuwait**. Other countries, including **Bahrain**, **Kiribati**, **Lao People's Democratic Republic**, **Namibia**, **Oman**, **Qatar** and **Solomon Islands**, are currently examining the Convention with a view to ratification.

Determinants of discrimination in remuneration

151. Women's lower human capital and intermittent career paths are widely believed to be the main reason for gender differentials in income. But, except for some countries of Africa and South Asia, the gender gap in primary and secondary schooling is not only narrowing worldwide, women's enrolment in higher education also equals or surpasses that of men.[14] And yet, women continue to hold lower-paying occupations than men with equivalent education and work experience. Labour market institutions are not a neutral arena, but reflect power relations in the economy and wider society. It is, therefore, important to explore the factors and processes that place women and other discriminated-against groups at the lower end of the pay structure. These are summarized in table 3.

Gender differentials in income

152. Determinants of gender-based inequalities in remuneration also include restrictions or prohibitions by law on women to work overtime or at night. Another factor relates to the perceived higher costs of employing a woman.[15] These costs include maternity protection benefits and the alleged higher

---

[14] United Nations: *The world's women 2000: Trends and statistics* (New York, 2000).

[15] ILO: *Report of the Committee of Experts on the Application of Conventions and Recommendations*, Report III(1A), International Labour Conference, 89th Session, Geneva, 2001, p. 19.

Table 3. Determinants of inequalities in remuneration for women and other social groups

Determining factors	Women	Race/ethnicity	Class/caste	Rural migrants	Young people	Elderly
Secondary earners	Nuclear family support; limited access to state benefits	Extended family support; low expected living standards	Low expected minimum living standards	Supported by family network in rural areas and in urban areas	Family support/ no state benefits	Pension support
Weak representation	Representation dominated by men; sectors difficult to organize	Representation dominated by main race/ethnic group	Representation may be dominated by skilled groups/higher castes	Not integrated into urban system of representation	Representation dominated by mature adults	Representation dominated by prime-age adults
Job segregation	Crowding into feminized jobs	Crowding by geographical area and by occupation	Status and pay of jobs reflects social class/caste hierarchy (including educational system)		Jobs designed and organized for young people	If only seeking part-time work may have to take jobs in female/youth sector
Social valuation of skills	Care work accorded low value	Skills associated with discriminated-against ethnic/racial groups may be accorded low value	Social valuation of skills may reflect class/caste status of workers	Rural skills accorded low value	Wage-for-age systems may devalue young workers' skills	Experience of older displaced workers accorded low value

Source: Adapted from J. Rubery: *Pay equity, minimum wage and equality at work*, Background paper prepared for this fourth Global Report (Manchester, University of Manchester Institute of Science and Technology, 2002).

absenteeism of women, lower propensity to work overtime, lower commitment to and interest in work and more limited mobility relative to men (see box 1.3).

153. The general lack of understanding of the distinction between the notion of equal remuneration for similar or equal work and equal remuneration for work of equal value, the elements of remuneration accounting for its assess-

---

Box 1.3

Do female workers cost more than male workers?

ILO research covering Argentina, Brazil, Chile, Mexico and Uruguay challenges the conventional belief that hiring a woman is more costly than hiring a man. The study shows that the additional cost of employing a woman worker and having to cover maternity protection and childcare expenses is very small as this component of non-wage costs amounts to less than 2% of the monthly gross earnings of women employees. If we consider *all* non-wage costs, including those of training and compensating work injuries and others, which apply to different categories of workers, both men and women, then the additional cost of hiring a woman comes down to less than 1 per cent.

This is as a result of the fact that the payment of maternity-related benefits and wages during maternity leave are not borne by the employers, but come out of taxes (Chile) or social security funding (Argentina, Brazil, Mexico and Uruguay). When funded by the social security system – which occurs in the majority of Latin American countries, except for Chile – the employer's contribution is not linked to the number or the age of women employees, but rather to the total number of employees of both sexes. This form of funding seeks to ensure an essential value: the protection of women against possible discrimination because of maternity, in the spirit of the ILO Conventions on maternity protection.

Source: L. Abramo and R. Todaro: *Cuestionando un mito: costos laborales de hombres y mujeres en América Latina* [Examining a myth: Labour costs for men and women in Latin America] (Lima, ILO, 2002).

ment and the methodology that can be employed to make an objective appraisal of jobs are important determinants that perpetuate pay inequality. Even neutral wage rates or wage categories, once established, can be applied to the disadvantage of women's income levels. For example, in **India**, wage classification of skilled and unskilled workers has sometimes placed women in the unskilled, lower-paying, wage category and men in the skilled, higher-paying, wage category, irrespective of the content or skill level of the job. [16]

154. Both employers and trade unions tend to give pay equity less priority than other issues, such as pay levels and employment. At a conference on equal pay for work of equal value in **Hong Kong, China,** in March 2000, a representative of the business sector concluded that redressing gender wage inequalities was a costly exercise entailing only marginal benefits. [17] Trade unions also tend to perceive pay equity as concerning women workers only and not as a matter of strategic interest for all workers. High unemployment rates and widespread poverty are often mentioned to justify inaction on this front. In transition economies, the occurrence of late or non-payment of wages is a motive for the low visibility of pay equity on trade union agendas. However, things are gradually changing. Public Services International (PSI) has launched a global campaign to promote pay equity among its affiliates. The main purpose of this campaign is to improve understanding about the issue and to build union capacity. Through training and advocacy work, PSI is promoting the inclusion of pay equity issues in collective bargaining.

Pay equity is less of a priority

155. The perceived cost of determining the extent of the pay gap and the resources needed to correct the imbalance act as a disincentive for trade unions and employers to tackle inequalities in remuneration. Low-cost methods, such as workplace pay audits, to identify pay inequalities have, however, been successfully tested. [18]

156. The growing prevalence of wage-setting systems based on workers' productivity or performance instead of on the content of the job raises new challenges for achieving pay equity. Additional payments related to experience, merit or performance are not equitably distributed to both high- and low-level employees. Furthermore, fringe benefits such as company cars are more common in men's contracts than in women's.

157. The lack of accurate and reliable statistics for measuring inequalities in remuneration are another impediment to achieving gender pay equity. At the workplace, the lack of data on wage rates for different groups of workers in different occupations and the secrecy surrounding this type of information hamper the conducting of job evaluation schemes.

Lack of accurate and reliable statistics

Trends in discrimination in remuneration

158. Earnings-related statistics tend to be disaggregated by sex more often than by race, colour or religion. Based on the limited and inadequate statistical evidence available, [19] no linear and uniform trend appears to exist regard-

No linear or uniform trend

---

[16] I. Mazumdar, R. Shankar Misra and A. Kapur: *Equal remuneration in India: Law and practice on gender-based wage differentials with special reference to the banking sector* (New Delhi, ILO, 2000).

[17] Equal Opportunities Commission Conference on Equal Pay for Work of Equal Value, Hong Kong, China, 18 March 2000. Presentation by P. Maule, Director of AON Consulting Hong Kong Ltd.

[18] J. Pillinger: *Pay equity now! Pay equity resource package* (Ferney-Voltaire, Public Services International, 2002), p. 20.

[19] Assessing trends in remuneration gaps is difficult because of the limited range of countries for which internationally comparable data sets exist, especially to measure changes over time. Moreover, the coverage of the different economic sectors and different occupations tends to be incomplete, with a clear bias favouring the urban formal sector.

ing gender imbalances in remuneration, but gender pay gaps are normally narrower in the public sector than in the private sector. Disparities in the average earnings of men and women vary by industry and country as a result of:

- *Differences in human capital endowments:* Investments in education, training, labour mobility and job search are generally lower for women than for men.

- *Horizontal occupational segregation by sex:* It appears that occupations mainly held by men have substantially higher pay rates as compared to those mainly held by women.

- *Vertical occupational segregation by sex:* Women tend to occupy lower ranks than men within the same occupation.

- *The necessity to reconcile work and family responsibilities:* Women may be forced or choose to accept jobs which enable them to combine family responsibilities with paid employment.

- *Work experience:* Women going in and out of the labour force gain less work experience, which induces lower wages.

- *Knowledge:* Information upon which to make comparisons or knowledge of rights and entitlements may be missing.

159. The gender gap in incomes has been narrowing in most places; nevertheless, it continues to be high although there are some significant exceptions.

160. In many industrialized and developing countries, the move of women into wider ranging and better-paid jobs has led to a rise in the earnings of the top decile of women compared to average income for men. This has resulted in greater gender equality, but at the cost of higher inequality between women, as the bulk of them remain concentrated in "women's jobs" that are low paid and low status. [20] Wage differentials are especially marked in those developing countries that are pursuing export-led industrialization or that have export processing zones. Disparity in earnings also extends to piece-work done at home and to most agricultural wage work.

161. The earnings gap tends to be smaller in countries that have centralized collective bargaining and that emphasize egalitarian wage policies in general (e.g. **Australia**, **Norway** and **Sweden**). It tends to be largest in countries that emphasize a traditional non-egalitarian role of women in the labour market (e.g. **Japan**) or that have decentralized market-oriented wage determination with enterprise-level bargaining (e.g. the **United States**). Pay differences between industries and between firms are generally greater under decentralized wage systems than under centralized wage systems. This means that wage system decentralization is likely to strengthen the effect of job segregation on pay differentials. [21]

Family/work reconciliation measures

162. In 1995, in all OECD countries, women's average incomes were lower than men's, with the biggest gap in **Japan** [22] and the **Republic of Korea**. [23] On a positive note, young and better-educated women have the lowest gender

---

[20] I. Bruegel and D. Perrons: "Deregulation and women's employment: The diverse experiences of women in Britain", in *Feminist Economics* (London, Routledge Journals), Vol. 4, No. 1, Spring 1998, pp. 103-125; and OECD: *Employment Outlook 2002* (Paris, 2002).

[21] F. Blau and L. Kahn: "Wage structure and gender earnings differentials: An international comparison", in *Economica* (Oxford, Blackwell Publishers), Vol. 63, No. 2509, 1996, pp. S29-S62.

[22] In 2002, female workers in Japan earned on average 65.5 per cent of average male wages. See International Confederation of Free Trade Unions: *Internationally recognised core labour standards in Japan*, Report for the WTO general council review of trade policies in Japan, Geneva, 6 and 8 November 2002, available at http:www.icftu.org/displaydocument.asp?Index =991216659&Language=EN

[23] OECD: *Employment Outlook 2001* (Paris, 2001), p. 139.

income gap, although this widens as age increases. Motherhood is an important determinant of income inequalities between the sexes and among women. This points to the importance of family/work reconciliation measures to facilitate women's participation in paid work.

163. Since the 1970s, the wage gap has been closing in OECD countries, although at a slow pace. In the past 15 years, the gap fell the most in the **United States** and **France**, where it decreased by 38 and 34 points, respectively, while **Sweden** and **Canada** displayed less rapid movement with a decrease of 14 and 15 points, respectively (see table 4). However, in **Sweden**, the biggest improvements in the gap had already been achieved in the 1970s. In the European Union, some studies estimate that at least 15 per cent of the pay gap is caused by direct or indirect discrimination. [24]

164. In the initial stages of the transition period in Central and Eastern European countries, there was apparent stability in the average gender pay gap. This hid important selection effects, such as the withdrawal of low-skilled and poorly paid women workers and the loss of work-related support services. [25] Since 1995, however, the data indicate a general tendency for the difference in average earnings between men and women to narrow, with a rise, in some countries, in the earnings of women relative to those of men. The largest increases seem to have occurred in countries such as **Poland, Romania and Slovenia**, where women's earnings were already relatively high compared to those of men. [26]

165. In Latin America, the ratio of average income per working hour between women and men in non-agricultural sectors increased from 68 per cent to 78 per cent between 1990 and 2000, while the monthly income ratio increased from 59 per cent to 66 per cent (see figure 5). The difference between these two indicators is due to the shorter working time average for women (39.9 weekly hours for women compared to 46.8 for men). This rise took place in the context of an increase in national GDPs, employment growth and "feminization" of the labour force. [27]

Table 4. The narrowing of the gender wage gap since the early 1980s, selected OECD countries
Gender wage gap (initial year = 100)

Country	Period	Index
Australia	1984-2001	82
Canada	1980-1999	85
France	1980-1999	66
Japan	1980-2000	81
Korea, Republic of	1977-1997	70
Portugal	1975-1999	70
Sweden	1975-1995	86
United Kingdom	1980-2000	70
United States	1979-1999	62

Source: OECD: *Employment Outlook 2002* (Paris, 2002).

---

[24] European Commission: *Gender Equality Magazine: Equal Pay*, No. 11 (Luxembourg, European Community Publications, 2001), p. 7.

[25] UNICEF: *Women in transition*, The MONEE Project, International Child Development Centre, Regional Monitoring Report No. 6 (Florence, UNICEF, 1999); and A. Newell and B. Reilly: *The gender pay gap in the transition from communism: Some empirical evidence*, William Davidson Institute Working Paper No. 305 (Brighton, University of Sussex, 2000).

[26] EUROSTAT: *Statistics in focus: Population and social conditions*, Theme 3, 5/2001 (European Communities), p. 6.

[27] ILO: *2001 Labour Overview* (Lima, 2001).

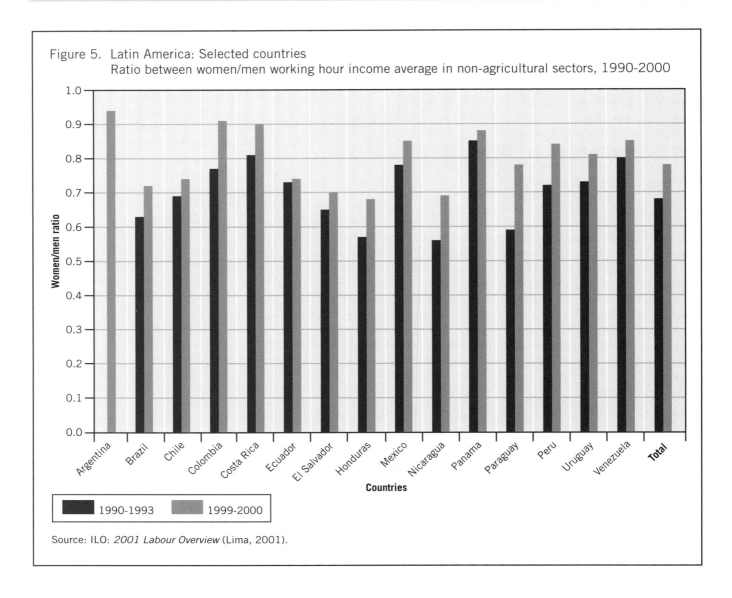

Figure 5. Latin America: Selected countries
Ratio between women/men working hour income average in non-agricultural sectors, 1990-2000

Source: ILO: *2001 Labour Overview* (Lima, 2001).

166. All countries reported an improvement in women's incomes relative to men's, the gains being largest in **Paraguay** (19 per cent) and **Colombia** (14 per cent) and more modest in countries such as **Chile** (5 per cent) and **Ecuador** (1 per cent).

Disparities in earnings based on race

The "racial penalty"   **167.** As mentioned earlier, there is little data available on discrimination against groups other than women. However, some information on differences in earnings based on race is available for the **United States**. This indicates that the "racial penalty":

— is greater for men than for women, which is explained by the greater occupational segregation between black/Hispanic men and white men than between black/Hispanic women and white women;[28]

---

[28] K. Bayard, J. Hellerstein, D. Neumark and K. Troske: *Why are racial and ethnic gaps larger for men than for women? Exploring the role of segregation using the new worker-establishment characteristics database*, National Bureau of Economic Research Working Paper No. 6997 (Cambridge, MA, 1999).

— is proportionally bigger at the top of the occupational hierarchy. The occupations with larger racial earnings disparities tended to be client-based professions that relied on social networks for their success while the smallest disparities were in those occupations for which pay depended little on the type of clients served; [29]

— increases with the level of education: more than half of the pay differences in hourly wages (almost 53 per cent) among black and white African immigrants who graduated from American universities [30] remained unexplained by earnings-related attributes such as education, occupation and hours worked.

168. In urban **Brazil**, white women have an average income that is higher than that of non-white men, but, once adjusted for the level of education, the work-income hierarchy is reversed and becomes non-white women at the bottom, white women, non-white men and white men at the top (see figure 6). [31] Although white women have the highest level of education of all population segments, including white men, they tend to be the most unemployed.

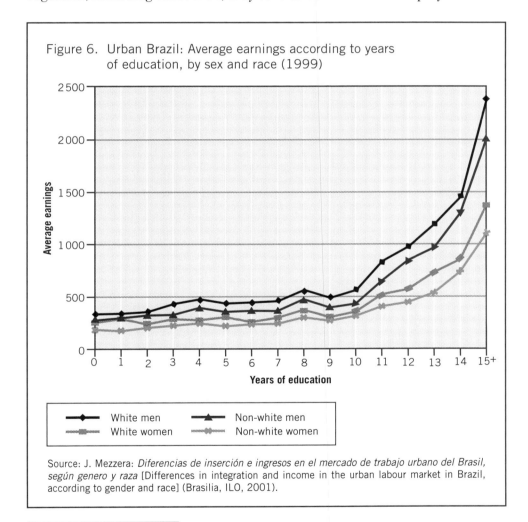

Figure 6. Urban Brazil: Average earnings according to years of education, by sex and race (1999)

Source: J. Mezzera: *Diferencias de inserción e ingresos en el mercado de trabajo urbano del Brasil, según genero y raza* [Differences in integration and income in the urban labour market in Brazil, according to gender and race] (Brasilia, ILO, 2001).

[29] E. Grodsky and D. Pager: "The structure of disadvantage: Individual and occupational determinants of the black-white wage gap", in *American Sociological Review* (Washington, DC, American Sociological Association), Vol. 66, No. 4, Aug. 2001.

[30] F. Nii-Amoo Dodoo and B.K. Takyi: "Africans in the diaspora: Black-white earnings differences among America's Africans", in *Ethnic and Racial Studies* (London, Routledge Taylor and Francis Group), Vol. 25, No. 6, Nov. 2002, pp. 913-941.

[31] J. Mezzera: *Diferencias de inserción e ingresos en el mercado de trabajo urbano del Brasil, según genero y raza* [Differences in integration and income in the urban labour market in Brazil, according to gender and race] (Brasilia, ILO, 2001).

The minimum wage

169. The adoption of a minimum wage policy, the primary goal of which is to set a floor for the wage structure in order to protect low wage earners, is designed to improve the earnings of those disproportionately represented at the bottom of the occupational hierarchy, i.e. women, migrants and other groups that may be discriminated against on the grounds of ethnicity, national origin, age, disability or health, among others.[32] The Government of **Bahrain,** for example, is considering introducing a minimum wage in the private sector that would apply to both national and expatriate workers. The latter comprise 60 per cent of the labour force and earn considerably less than do national workers. This measure would be a positive step towards the elimination of discrimination between national and migrant labour.[33]

Women benefit from minimum wage policies

170. There is some information on how women have actually benefited from a minimum wage in this respect. In Eastern and Central Europe, economic restructuring took different forms in different countries, but a common feature was that the earnings of both men and women were dragged down, and, for many, earnings ended up being well below subsistence levels. In countries such as **Poland**, however, where the minimum wage was kept at a reasonable level, it has contributed to maintaining relatively equal wages in the state sector and has reduced the incidence of low pay.

171. In the **Netherlands**, the national system of collective bargaining builds upon the minimum wage policy and sets legally enforceable wage rates and conditions in many sectors where women are employed. As of 1993, the scope of the minimum wage was extended to include workers working for less than a third of the standard week. This move reduced the incidence of low pay among this group of workers, where women are strongly represented.[34] The **United Kingdom** introduced a national minimum wage in April 1999, with benefits for gender pay equity, particularly for part-time workers. Women accounted for 70 per cent of those who benefited from this measure and over two-thirds of this total were part-time workers. Other groups included ethnic minorities, particularly the Pakistani and Bangladeshi communities, as well as manual workers. In the **United States,** the federal minimum wage has been evolving in real and relative terms since 1968, reaching its peak value in the second half of the 1990s. Women have benefited relatively more from this rise as they account for 65 per cent of the total. The share of black workers among the beneficiaries was 15.1 per cent, compared to 11.6 per cent workforce share, and the share of Hispanics was 17.4 per cent, compared to 10.6 per cent workforce share. The majority of minimum wage beneficiaries were part-time workers, but full-time workers still accounted for 48 per cent of those affected, while 40 per cent were the sole breadwinners.[35]

172. A minimum wage policy is often considered irrelevant to the self-employed, the majority of whom are women workers in many developing countries. Some evidence suggests, however, that a minimum wage has the merit of setting a reference earnings target for workers in the informal economy. In

---

[32] J. Rubery: *Pay equity, minimum wage and equality at work.* Background paper prepared for this fourth Global Report (Manchester, University of Manchester Institute of Science and Technology, 2002).

[33] ILO: *Employment, social protection and social dialogue: An integrated policy framework for promoting decent work in Bahrain*, Report of the Interdisciplinary Mission on Employment Promotion and Social Protection in Bahrain (26-30 January and 26-27 February 2002) (Geneva, 2002).

[34] J. Plantenga, E. Koch and M. Sloep: *Trends and prospects for women's employment in the 1990s: The case of the Netherlands*, Working paper from the European Commission Women's Employment Project, European Work and Employment Research Centre (Manchester, University of Manchester Institute of Science and Technology, 1996).

[35] J. Rubery, op. cit., pp. 58-59.

Indonesia, a survey of managers in the footwear and garment trades found general compliance, with men paid well above the minimum wage and women paid at minimum wage levels. Management viewed red tape and bureaucracy associated with export licences to be more problematic than minimum wages. [36] In other instances, some small and low-productivity enterprises operating on the fringes of formality may comply only partially with a minimum wage policy and uphold the payment of non-wage benefits such as paid holidays, sick leave or retirement benefits in order to reduce costs. [37]

173. It may be argued that a minimum wage, with adequate determination and adjustment mechanisms, helps to reduce wage dispersions, and the gender income gap tends to be narrower where wage dispersion is lower. The challenges of adopting a minimum wage as a device to narrow gender inequalities in respect of remuneration are manifold, as are the opportunities. In contexts where trade unions are not well represented, it may constitute a useful component of any approach towards achieving gender pay equity.

The challenges of adopting a minimum wage

[36] L.P. Rosner: "The impact of recent increases in minimum wage rates on employment growth and poverty in Indonesia", unpublished manuscript referred to in M. Rama: "The consequences of doubling the minimum wage: The case of Indonesia" in *Industrial and Labour Relations Review* (New York, Cornell Universtiy), Vol. 54, No. 4, July 2001, pp. 864-881.

[37] Y. van der Meulen Rodgers: *Protecting women and promoting equality in the labour market: Theory and evidence*, Policy research report on gender and development, Working Paper Series, No. 6 (World Bank Development Research Group, 1999).

2. Policy issues and interventions

174. There are a number of policies that are considered important to overcoming discrimination: legislation, enforcement, affirmative action, relevant data, education and training, and employment services. While all of these fall within the mandate of the ILO – and the ILO has cooperated with the constituents in some of these – the purpose here is to highlight these issues and interventions and not the ILO's work, which is addressed later. However, this should not prevent the reader from drawing conclusions with regard to where further efforts by the ILO and other international partners may be required.

175. Whatever the form of discrimination, its elimination requires a similar set of policy devices that range from consistent and adequate legislation and affirmative action measures to suitable training and employment policies and programmes. What tends to change is the mix of policy interventions, and the relative importance of each policy device at different stages.

Legislation: An indispensable first step

The role of the State 176. The State plays a key role in the elimination of discrimination and the realization of equality at work. Legislation can contribute to achieving this goal: directly, by addressing the problem of discrimination at work (see table 5), and indirectly, by guaranteeing equality in matters other than work. These include family life, inheritance, property and contractual rights, access to land and credit, and education. In countries where there is legal pluralism, the creation of an equality legal environment must also concern customary law.

177. In common law countries, the judiciary plays an important role in the development of anti-discrimination law. In **India**, the Supreme Court handed down a ruling that included guidelines and norms prohibiting sexual harassment in the workplace. [38] In **Zimbabwe**, a Labour Court handed down a ruling in support of a claim of sexual harassment despite the lack of relevant legal provisions. [39]

178. Some countries, including **Finland** and the **Netherlands**, also rely on criminal law to address discrimination at work.

---

[38] N. Haspels, Z.M. Kasim, C. Thomas and D. McCann: *Action against sexual harassment at work in Asia and the Pacific* (Bangkok, ILO, 2001), p. 70.

[39] ibid., p. 70.

Table 5.   The types of legislation that include anti-discrimination provisions [a]

Types of legislation	Scope	Examples
Constitution	— General equality principle	Almost all countries
	— Prohibition of discrimination at work	Brazil
	— Equal pay	Brazil, Ecuador, Italy, Switzerland
	— Positive action	India, Namibia, South Africa
Labour law	— Prohibition of discrimination	Benin, Russian Federation
	— Positive action	France
	— Equal pay	Benin, Chad
Non-discrimination and equality law	— Only employment	Denmark (Act on Prohibition of Differential Treatment on the Labour Market), Guyana (Prevention of Discrimination Act)
	— Employment and other socio-economic issues	Trinidad and Tobago (Equal Opportunity Act)
	— Only one ground of discrimination	United Kingdom (Sex Discrimination Act, Race Relations Act, Disability Discrimination Act)
	— Several grounds or social groups	Guyana (Prevention of Discrimination Act), Ireland (Employment Equality Act), United States (Title VII of the Civil Rights Act of 1964)
	— Positive action	Canada (Employment Equity Act), Italy (Act. 125 providing for affirmative action to achieve equal treatment of men and women in employment), Namibia (Affirmative Action (Employment) Act), South Africa (Employment Equity Act)

[a] This table provides an idea of the types of legislation and non-discrimination provisions that exist at present to combat discrimination in employment and occupation, and examples of some of the countries that have adopted them. It is not comprehensive, nor is it representative of the "best law examples".

179. Equal pay legislation has been widely used to combat discrimination in respect of remuneration between men and women. While equal pay legislation addresses the undervaluation of jobs done predominantly by women and gender biases in pay structures and wage-fixing mechanisms, it does not tackle the many other factors that contribute to the difference in women's pay relative to men's; hence the need for complementary equal opportunity legislation or for equality legislation that provides the duty to promote equality more generally. In **Sweden**, the Equal Opportunities Act requires that employers who have at least ten employees draw up annual plans of action for promoting equality that include pay matters and action to redress inequalities in this respect. Moreover, certain countries have also adopted civil service statutes addressing discrimination and promoting equality of opportunity in state employment.

Equal pay legislation

180. Public service statutes can also address discrimination in employment. The Public Service (Amendment) Act in **Botswana** and the General Civil Servants' Regulations in **France** contain provisions protecting against sexual harassment in the public service. In **Brazil**, the Federal Public Service Act tackles discrimination faced by people with disabilities by reserving for them 20 per cent of the vacant posts open to competition in the federal public service. [40]

181. With regard to anti-discrimination or equality legislation, two approaches have been pursued. The first consists of dealing with race, sex, dis-

Anti-discrimination or equality legislation

[40] J. Hodges-Aeberhard: *Comparative study of contents of civil service statutes*, Department for Government and Labour Law and Administration, Document No. 5 (Geneva, ILO, 2001), pp. 37-38.

ability and other grounds of discrimination through separate anti-discrimination legal regimes and separate law-enforcing mechanisms and institutions, as in the **United Kingdom**. The second consists of a single anti-discrimination or equality law that seeks to eliminate various unlawful grounds of discrimination, as in **Australia** and the **United States**. Either approach has its advantages and raises certain challenges. Country circumstances and priorities determine which type of regulatory framework might best serve the goal of eliminating discrimination at work. In any approach, it is important that the regulatory framework be clear, consistent and equitable, and that it encourage the responsibility of enterprises and individuals to promote equality.

Shifts in legal approaches to combat discrimination and promote equality

A positive duty to promote equality

182. A growing number of countries have moved away from a legal approach exclusively based on the imposition of the negative duty not to discriminate to a broader one encompassing a positive duty to prevent discrimination and promote equality. While an anti-discrimination legal model based on prohibiting discriminatory practices has proven successful in eliminating the most blatant forms of discrimination, such as direct pay discrimination,[41] it has encountered less success with the more subtle forms, such as occupational segregation.[42] Moreover, its effectiveness in eliminating discrimination is heavily dependent on litigation and this prevents it from reaching those workers who are the most disadvantaged and vulnerable to discrimination. These workers tend not to make use of the law to have redress because of ignorance or fear of retaliation.

Mainstreaming equality concerns

183. In more recent years, there has been a trend towards mainstreaming equality concerns in general policy and law-making. For example, in the **Czech Republic**, the 1998 National Action Plan, Government Priorities and Procedures in Promoting Equality between Men and Women, and the 1999 National Employment Plan both indicate gender mainstreaming, to which all ministers are bound, as one of the fundamental policy tools to promote equal opportunities for men and women. In Northern Ireland, section 75 of the Northern Ireland Act of 1998 provides for mainstreaming religious equality policies by requiring public authorities to have due regard, in carrying out their functions, to the need to promote equality of opportunity between persons of different religious belief. Mainstreaming entails an assessment of the likely impact of proposed legislation and policies on distinct groups, such as women or minorities, and their involvement in the relevant decision-making processes.[43] Mainstreaming needs to be seen as a complement to, rather than a substitute for, specific anti-discrimination legislation in order to ensure that specific equality concerns do not get diluted.

184. Equal opportunity laws adopted by supranational bodies or in the framework of regional trade agreements may influence the development of relevant national legislation. For example, CARICOM has adopted, as part of its project on harmonization of labour legislation, a model legislation on equality of op-

---

[41] See D. Neumark and W. Stock: *The effects of race and sex discrimination laws*, Working Paper 8215, NBER working paper series (Cambridge, MA, National Bureau of Economic Research, 2001), available at http://www.nber.org/papers/w8215.

[42] L. Dickens: "Anti-discrimination legislation: Exploring and explaining the impact on women's employment", in W. McCarthy (ed.): *Legal intervention in industrial relations: Gains and losses* (Oxford, Blackwell Publishing, 1992), pp. 103-146).

[43] C. McCrudden: "Regulating discrimination: Advice to a legislator on problems regarding the enforcement of anti-discrimination law and strategies to overcome them", in T. Loenen and P.R. Rodrigues (eds.): *Non-discrimination law: Comparative perspectives* (The Hague, Kluwer Law International, 1999), pp. 310-311.

portunity and treatment for women in employment to guide law-making in Member States. European equality law, which covers issues such as equal pay, social security, occupational pension schemes, maternity protection, parental leave and part-time work, [44] has a direct bearing on national equality laws. More recently, Council Directive 2000/78/EC lays down a general framework for combating discrimination on the grounds of religion or belief, disability, age or sexual orientation as regards employment and occupation with a view to putting into effect in the Member States the principle of equal treatment. [45] The scope of European Union law and related jurisprudence is expanding, as prospective new Member States of the Union have to transpose into their systems the Community *acquis,* which includes equality law and jurisprudence. [46]

Public procurement policies: A new instrument to promote equality?

185. Public procurement is increasingly used at the national level to complement legislation in furthering social goals. [47] Particularly in Europe and North America, public procurement policies have been put in place to tackle the problem of discrimination faced by certain groups, including women, ethnic or religious minorities and the disabled. In **South Africa**, the Preferential Procurement Policy Framework Act of 2000 provides that "an organ of state must determine its preferential procurement policy" and establish a system whereby points are allocated for specific goals. These may include "contracting with persons, or categories of persons, historically disadvantaged by unfair discrimination on the basis of race, gender or disability" (article 2).

Public procurement policies complement legislation

186. The public bodies involved in public procurement policies may be central governmental departments, regional or local governments. In some instances, the relevant costs are completely left to enterprises; in others, the contracting authority provides contractors with advice or financial subsidies. Only occasionally are subcontractors encompassed. The growing reliance on subcontracting arrangements limits, therefore, the impact of public procurement policies along the supply chain. Other instruments, such as codes of conduct and international framework agreements, have been increasingly adopted to overcome these limitations (see Part III, Chapter 2).

Enforcement, monitoring and promotion are crucial for sustained change

187. Effective enforcement of any law requires government investment in human and financial resources, establishment and operation of administrative and judicial structures, knowledge about the subject matter of the law, and

---

[44] Article 4 of Council Directive 97/80/EC of 15 December 1997 on the burden of proof in cases of discrimination based on sex reads: "when persons who consider themselves wronged because the principle of equal treatment has not been applied to them establish, before a court or other competent authority, facts from which it may be presumed that there has been direct or indirect discrimination, it shall be for the respondent to prove that there has been no breach of the principle of equal treatment".

[45] Council Directive 2000/78/EC of 27 November 2000 establishing a general framework for equal treatment in employment and occupation (article 1). Consistent with European equality law, the directive lays down that it shall be for the respondent to prove that there has been no breach of the principle of equal treatment (article 10).

[46] The Community *acquis* is the body of common rights and obligations that binds all the Member States together within the European Union. Applicant countries have to accept the Community *acquis* before they can join the European Union.

[47] C. McCrudden: "Social policy issues in public procurement: A legal overview", in S. Arrowsmith and A. Davies (eds.): *Public procurement: Global revolution* (The Hague, Kluwer Law International, 1998), pp. 219-239.

worker and employer confidence in the system. Most enforcement systems are complaints-based and thus rely on individual workers, their representatives or administrative officials to trigger their operation. Denial of equal opportunities, treatment or dignity at work require particularly responsive enforcement systems to ensure that equality laws are applied to all workers, especially those who are members of minority groups or women.

188. There are many challenges in enforcing the law. For example, victims of discrimination find it hard to obtain adequate legal assistance and representation, to get to court or to understand the proceedings, to handle long delays, to pay high costs and to gather enough evidence to prove their cases. This may be coupled with lack of knowledge of equality principles, gender and cultural issues among lawyers and judges, inadequate settlements, remedies and sanctions, and poorly resourced special enforcement bodies or courts with insufficient staff and inadequate procedures and powers.

189. Many governments recognize the need to strengthen their equality enforcement mechanisms. To do so, they continue to revise their labour or equality laws by extending their scope, increasing remedies and sanctions, changing procedural rules, strengthening the labour inspectorate or establishing and strengthening administrative and judicial bodies.

The labour inspectorate – a key enforcement body

190. Labour inspectors are responsible for the enforcement of equality provisions where such provisions exist in general labour law or specific equal employment laws. The advisory functions of the labour inspectorate can play a role in preventing or overcoming discrimination, and they may be able to contribute to the effective resolution of discrimination cases and play a role in assisting other enforcement bodies. Unfortunately, most labour inspectorates are short of financial, infrastructure and human resources. They are often overburdened with diverse responsibilities and have little training in discrimination.

191. Some governments have provided specialized training and awareness raising to broaden the competencies of the labour inspectorate to prevent, monitor and punish direct and indirect discriminatory practices, including sexual harassment and wage discrimination. The new Equal Pay Act of 2002 of **Cyprus** gives a specific role to the labour inspectorate on equal pay inspections and establishes a technical committee to undertake an evaluation of equal value in the case of complaints. In **Brazil**, state level inspectorates specializing in discrimination have been established. In the **Philippines**, questions on discrimination have been included in inspection lists.

Specialized enforcement bodies

192. Countries have made efforts to tackle discrimination and promote equality through the creation of specialized enforcement bodies. These bodies may be generally categorized into two types. The first type is advisory and promotional, and may include commissions on the advancement of women, minority councils and inter-ministerial coordination bodies. These bodies usually collect, publish and disseminate information, analyse and advise on legislation, policy and implementing plans of action, and provide training. Their structure is often "tripartite-plus" in order to include representatives of the main stakeholder groups. In **Uruguay**, the Tripartite Commission on Equal Opportunities and Treatment in Employment is composed of representatives of workers, employers, the Ministry of Labour and Social Security and the National Institute for Family and Women's Affairs. It provides assistance and disseminates information on equal opportunity legislation. The second type has quasi-judicial powers, allowing it to examine complaints on discrimination. Some bodies, such as the Human Rights and Equal Opportunity Commission in **Australia**, have both promotional and monitoring powers. Some complaint-based bodies deal with discrimination in a wide number of areas (e.g. education, employment, housing), while others address only employment discrimination (e.g. in **Austria, Brazil** and Northern Ireland). Many bodies focus on the protection

of a particular group, such as women or ethnic minorities, while others cover more than one social group or multiple grounds of discrimination (e.g. in **Hong Kong (China), Trinidad and Tobago** and the **United States**). A recent initiative has been the establishment of national commissions on human rights, which usually cover employment discrimination, in **Ghana, Pakistan** and **South Africa**. The advantage of bodies that deal only with discrimination against a particular group, such as women or minorities, is that they can become specialized in all aspects of that ground of discrimination. However, those that cover more grounds of discrimination are better equipped to handle a variety of aspects and multiple forms of discrimination.

193. Specialized enforcement bodies can assist victims of discrimination in the handling and resolution of their complaints in an informal and inexpensive manner. The claims procedures are generally more accessible to the ordinary person than going to court and they respond to the sensitive nature of complex discrimination cases. In **Ghana, Hong Kong (China)** and the **United States**, agencies also have the power to initiate complaints and investigations themselves and need not rely on individual complaints.

Assisting victims of discrimination

194. Improving the effectiveness of these mechanisms entails addressing limitations on their authority or powers, lack of funding and appropriate staffing, lack of accessibility to those who need them most and, above all, the political will to support their enforcement actions. Ways to increase accessibility could include the creation of regional or local offices or the provision of "mobile institutions", and the simplification of procedures. While the creation of specialized complaints bodies can be considered a positive trend, their multiplicity, overlapping mandates and lack of coordination may raise problems of effective enforcement. **Canada** is one of the countries that has put a mechanism in place to address discrimination based on a variety of grounds in employment, as well as in other spheres.

195. Ombudspersons or ombudsperson-type offices have two primary roles: (1) to investigate maladministration, and (2) to provide remedies where injustice is found. Their purpose is to make recommendations, assessments and criticisms and to submit an annual report to parliament. In some countries, offices of ombudspersons have been created to address equality issues. In **Hungary**, ombudspersons are competent to investigate cases and institute proceedings before the court, or to join constitutional complaints lodged by individuals.

The office of the Ombudsperson

196. Within the judicial framework, formal complaints of employment discrimination may be brought to labour tribunals or courts, as well as to civil courts from municipal level to the Supreme Court of the nation. Proving discrimination in formal proceedings is difficult even when intent does not have to be shown. In most cases involving hiring, firing, pay and promotion decisions, it is the employer who possesses the relevant information on the decision-making. In sexual harassment cases, there are often no witnesses. To assist claimants and to allow for a fair hearing, a growing number of countries are shifting the burden of proof to the employer to disprove the allegations once the claimant has made a first showing of discrimination. An area that offers a particular challenge to courts is the enforcement of equal remuneration laws. To assist the employment tribunals in the **United Kingdom** in addressing this issue, job evaluation experts are assigned to equal pay cases and provide the tribunal members with technical advisory reports.

Legal action

Closing the gap: Affirmative action

197. The expression "affirmative action" refers to: "a coherent packet of measures, of a temporary character, aimed specifically at correcting the position of members of a target group in one or more aspects of their social life, in

Affirmative action measures for designated groups

order to obtain effective equality".[48] In some countries, such as the **United States**, where this expression originated in the 1960s, these measures are called affirmative action measures. In **Canada**, the Employment Equity Act of 1996 refers to these measures as employment equity measures, where employment equity means: "more than treating people in the same way but also requires special measures and the accommodation of differences" (article 2). Throughout Europe, the expression "positive action" is used and, in yet other countries, the expression is "special temporary measures". In **South Africa**, the Employment Equity Act of 1998 defines affirmative action measures as "measures designed to ensure that suitably qualified people from designated groups have equal employment opportunities and are equitably represented in all occupational categories and levels in the workforce of a designated employer" (article 15).

198. Irrespective of the terminology used, these policy measures aim to accelerate the pace of participation of members of under-represented groups in gaining access to jobs, education, training and promotion, among other things. These measures may consist of giving some advantage to members of target groups, where there is a very narrow margin of difference between job applicants, or of granting substantial preference to members of designated groups. Employment equity plans, setting goals and timetables for increasing the representation of beneficiary groups and indicating the policies needed for their realization are examples of these types of measures. Quota systems allocating a proportion of certain positions for members of designated groups also fall under the label of affirmative action measures.

Temporary nature of affirmative action measures

199. A common feature of affirmative action measures is their temporary nature. This presupposes a regular and objective evaluation of affirmative action programmes aimed at ascertaining their effectiveness, redefining regularly their scope and content and determining when to bring them to an end. In some countries, however, they may be discontinued or their effectiveness reduced as a result of cuts in social spending, economic downturns or economic restructuring. In other countries, such as **India**, they have acquired a permanent or semi-permanent character.

200. To avoid unintended backlash and the stigmatization of designated groups, it is important to obtain their prior consent and to engage in consultations with all the stakeholders concerned. The stakeholders comprise the economically dominant groups as well as potential beneficiaries, the State, at different levels, and employers' and workers' organizations. The potential and actual effects of the application of these policies on third parties should be anticipated and monitored. Employment equity consultations of the kind conducted in Regina and Saskatoon, **Canada**, in 2001, to discuss the roles and responsibilities of different government and non-government parties in achieving employment equity and ways of measuring success are noteworthy.[49] Positive action measures must be defined flexibly and in line with changes in people's ideas and perceptions, and compatibly with national cultural circumstances, socio-political realities and economic possibilities.[50]

---

[48] United Nations Economic and Social Council: *Prevention of discrimination: The concept and practice of affirmative action*, Final Report submitted by M. Bossuyt, Special Rapporteur, in accordance with resolution 1998/5 of the Sub-Commission on the Promotion and Protection of Human Rights, doc. E/CN.4/Sub.2/2002/21, 17 June 2002, p. 3.

[49] Saskatchewan Human Rights Commission: *Annual Report 2000-2001: Promoting dignity and equality for all*, Chapter on "Employment equity", available at http://www.gov.sk.cs/shrc/annreport2001/default.htm

[50] J. Hodges-Aeberhard and C. Raskin (eds.): *Affirmative action in the employment of ethnic minorities and persons with disabilities* (Geneva, ILO, 1997).

Box 2.1

Affirmative action in India:
A complex process of negotiating change in a democratic polity

Affirmative action in India is aimed at redressing social backwardness – a move based on a constitutional mandate to address the problem of social inequality faced by innumerable castes and tribes. Caste-based social stratification is not confined to Hindu society (around 80 per cent of the population); it has also influenced other religious communities such as Muslim, Christian and Sikh. The official designation of those entitled to affirmative action is Backward Classes. This is subdivided into two groups: (i) SC/ST, i.e. Scheduled Castes (the former "untouchable" castes, now forming around 15 per cent of the population) and Scheduled Tribes (the tribes who were outside the caste system and lived in forests and mountainous areas, forming around 8 per cent of the population), (ii) OBC, i.e. Other Backward Castes (a number of cultivating and artisan castes about whom there is no census enumeration but who are estimated to comprise from 25 to 50 per cent of the population). All religious communities are included in this classification.

Affirmative action, better known in India as Reservation Policy, seeks to reserve seats in elected political bodies, government jobs and educational institutions mainly for SC and ST. The highly contested issue is that of job reservation. Since 1951, the central (federal) government reserves 22 per cent of its jobs for SC (15 per cent) and ST (7 per cent) candidates. Of late, communities not covered by the Reservation Policy increasingly resent it. Some see it as a compromise on efficiency (merit). As an effective alternative to the reservation policy, many scholars argue for increasing access to education and improving its quality as a social leveller in the long run. But governments, especially at the state level, lack political commitment in widening educational opportunities at the school level despite the manifest benefits of such a strategy in social levelling in the State of Kerala.

Source: A. Béteille: "The conflict of norms and values in contemporary Indian society", in P.L. Berger (ed.): *The limits of social cohesion: Conflict and mediation in pluralist societies* (Boulder, CO, Westview Press, 1998), pp. 265-292.

201. The number and types of groups that benefit from these measures tend to change over time and across countries. In **Canada**, an initial commitment to affirmative action for women was later complemented by a concern for employment equity for four distinct groups: women, indigenous peoples, the disabled and the "visible minorities".[51] In **India** (see box 2.1), the list of groups entitled to reservation policies has been the subject of regular reviews. In the **United States**, growing demographic diversity has recently led to the inclusion of immigrant workers among the beneficiaries of affirmative action measures.[52]

202. The determination of who is entitled to these measures is key since it has clear implications, inter alia, for budgeting decisions, but this is not always an easy task. The heated debate as to which groups in **Brazil** should benefit from the introduction of affirmative action policies to combat racial discrimination was linked in part to the "fuzziness" of the concept of colour.

Who should benefit

---

[51] The term "visible minorities" is used to describe people of immigrant origin. See C.L. Bacchi: *The politics of affirmative action: Women, equality and category politics* (London, SAGE Publications, 1996).

[52] D.R. Harris and R. Farley: "Demographic, economic and social trends and projections", in J.S. Jackson (ed.): *New directions: African Americans in a diversifying nation* (Washington, DC, National Policy Association, 2000).

Has affirmative action brought about the intended results?

203. In a number of cases, affirmative, or positive, action has redressed labour market inequalities between dominant and designated groups [53] and raised productivity and stock returns of enterprises. In Northern Ireland, where such measures have been in force since 1989, employment segregation has narrowed and the under-representation of the Catholic community overall and of Catholic and Protestant communities in specific areas has declined as well. [54] In **South Africa**, the number of black households earning as much or more than the average white household has risen from less than 1,000 to 1.2 million in less than a decade. [55] Affirmative action seems also to generate some positive unintended effects. For instance, minority doctors are more likely than doctors from the dominant groups to treat low-income or minority patients.

204. The impact of affirmative, or positive, action appears to vary across countries (see table 6), and even within countries, depending on the grounds giving rise to discrimination and its manifestations. For example, in the **United States**, progress on gender equality has been greater overall than that on racial equality. [56] The Nordic countries have been more successful than other OECD countries in reducing inequities in remuneration between men and women, but have been less effective in addressing occupational segregation. Empirical evidence suggests that the impact of affirmative action on the performance of employees belonging to a designated group depends on how it is implemented. In the **United States**, "affirmative action employers" have more effective screening methods that permit them to uncover unobservable characteristics of potential recruits. [57] They also have more focused training and evaluation techniques that enable them to help minority employees improve their qualifications.

No negative effect on productivity

205. A recent study covering **Australia** and the **United Kingdom** showed that equal opportunity measures have no negative effect on productivity in either country, even among groups of enterprises where these policies are, in principle, almost compulsory. [58] Among large enterprises, in particular, the effects on productivity were generally positive and statistically significant in both countries. This shows not only that it is feasible to have strong legislation making it compulsory for enterprises to adopt affirmative action measures, but also that enforcing this legislation carefully and encouraging enterprises to make a commitment to affirmative action measures may be a viable strategy.

206. Generally, the decline in employment or occupational inequalities between "mainstream" groups and "target" groups has not been accompanied by a proportional decline in inequalities among the beneficiary groups themselves. To ensure more equal results, some analysts have suggested taking into account group membership, as well as socio-economic status and

---

[53] J. Hodges-Aeberhard and C. Raskin (eds.), op. cit.

[54] B. Hepple: *Work, empowerment and equality* (Geneva, ILO, 2000), pp. 4-6.

[55] International Council on Human Rights Policy: *Racial and economic exclusion: Policy implications* (Versoix, 2001), p. 10.

[56] W.A. Darity Jr. and P.L. Mason: "Evidence on discrimination in employment: Codes of color, codes of gender", in *The Journal of Economic Perspectives* (Nashville, TN, American Economic Association), Vol. 12, No. 2, 1998, pp. 63-90.

[57] H. Holzer and D. Neumark: "Assessing affirmative action", op. cit. The authors argue that the heavy reliance on screening by employers embracing affirmative action measures permits them to uncover other unobservable characteristics of the minority workers that compensate for their lower educational achievements.

[58] It is plausible to expect slightly negative effects on productivity of enterprises for which these policies are compulsory, since enterprises that found these policies to be costly would not be able to abandon them and other enterprises may have incentives to put up "cosmetic" policies.

Table 6.   Fighting racial discrimination: Affirmative action policy in selected countries

Country	Ethnic groups	% of total population	Inequalities before affirmative action	Affirmative action	Outcome	Comments
Malaysia	Bumiputras Chinese Indians	62 30 8	Bumiputra held political power; Chinese held economic power. Mean income of Chinese was 2.29 that of Malays and mean income of Indians was 1.77 that of Malays. In 1970, among student enrolled in tertiary education, there were 49.7% Malay, 42.7% Chinese and 5.1% Indians. Incidence of poverty: 49% in 1970.	The New Economic Policy (1970) aimed to reduce and eventually eliminate the identification of race with economic function. It also aimed to eradicate poverty regardless of race. Types of policies included quotas, targets and affirmative action in favour of the Bumiputras with respect to: – education – land ownership – public service employment – ownership of corporate companies.	Gap in average income has narrowed but has not been eliminated. In 1995, mean income of Chinese was 1.81 that of Malays and mean income of Indians was 1.35 that of Malays. Between 1970 and 1995, the share of Bumiputras among: – professionals rose from 8% to 54% – university students rose from 43% to 54% – ownership of corporate companies rose from 1.5% to 20.6%. Incidence of poverty: 7.5% in 1999.	The rapid economic growth (6.7% between 1970 and 1990) helped the State to pursue its ethnic redistributive policy. The segmentation of the labour market persists and Bumiputras are seriously under-represented in the professional and technical categories and in the private manufacturing and service sectors. Ethnic discrimination primarily involves the business community and the middle class, and tensions subsist.
Brazil	Whites Afro-Brazilians Mixed race Others Racial categories are fluid: continuum of colour from white to black	54 5 40 1	Large inequalities in incomes, occupations, education, mortality rates and political positions. They coincide with the racial continuum. In 1996, black family income was 43% that of a white family and years of schooling was 63% that of a white family.	Fighting social disadvantage was through poverty alleviation measures. Educational measures to help blacks and the needy to university entrance, setting targets for the proportion of blacks in education and in government positions. In 2002, a quota system was introduced in the civil service.	Inequalities proved difficult to alter in the 1990s. Even after controlling for education and region, white workers still have an income that is 20% higher than that of black workers. Women earn 60% of men's salaries. It is too early to assess the impact of new measures.	The "fuzziness" of racial categories makes group targeting difficult. The wide dispersion of income hampers narrowing differentials between groups.
South Africa (post-apartheid)	Africans Whites Coloureds Asians	75 14 9 2	Africans have the political majority but face large and adverse horizontal inequalities. In 1990, the average monthly salary of black workers was 29% that of white workers. State expenditure on education per white student was 14 times that per black student.	New policies aim to reduce black/white differentials in the field of education and employment. The Employment Equity Act (1998) was a policy of affirmative action in favour of African, Asian and coloured people through preferential treatment and numerical goals. The Skills Development Act (1998) compels employers to implement training measures for people from disadvantaged groups.	Racial differentials have been diminishing but remain extremely high. Unemployment rates for 2001: Whites: 6% Africans: 36% Coloureds: 22% Indians: 18%. The proportion of blacks in managerial posts in the public sector rose to 35% by 1998. The share of black business in stock market capitalization rose to 6% in 2000.	The economic liberalization agenda imposes limits on government expenditure and constrains redistributive policies. Black unemployment has been rising. Colour-barring employment practices favouring white workers are still practised through informal screening devices. There is a substantial gender gap.
United States	Whites Blacks American Indians Others (of which are Hispanos/Latinos)	82 13 1 4 (12)	1970 differentials: – median income of black households was 60% that of white households – in life expectancy between whites and blacks were 8 years for men and 7.3 years for women – college graduates 10.3% among white men, 3% among black men, 6% among white women, 3% among black women. Population below poverty line in 1980: White: 10% Black: 33% Hispanic: 26%.	Affirmative action in the field of employment, education and housing aimed at increasing opportunities for black workers. Obligation for federal contractors to take affirmative action in favour of minority and vulnerable groups.	The programmes had a positive though not very large impact. Gains were relatively bigger in some blue-collar and white-collar occupations. But discrimination of many kinds persists and inequalities between groups remain large. Unemployment of blacks is double that of whites; infant mortality rate is twice as high. Population below poverty line in 2000: White: 10% Black: 24% Asian: 11% Hispanic: 23%.	The 1964 Civil Rights Act initiated some affirmative measures. In the 1980s, enforcement lapsed. It was reasserted with the Civil Rights Act of 1991, which strengthened existing civil rights laws and provided for damages in case of intentional employment discrimination. Dispersion of income has increased in the 1990s.

Sources: United States Bureau of the Census: *Statistical Abstract of the United States: 121st edition* (Washington, DC, 2001); Brazilian Institute of National Statistics and Geography (IBGE) and Brazilian Institute of Applied Economic Research (IPEA); Malaysian Economic Planning Unit (EPU) five-year and long-term development plans; Statistics South Africa.

other characteristics, when determining who qualifies for positive action measures. [59]

207. The necessity for, and legitimacy of, affirmative action measures has been a matter of controversy. Detractors argue that these measures constitute a form of positive or reverse discrimination, in that they generate unfair preferential treatment of members of certain groups on the basis of characteristics, such as race or religion, that should be considered irrelevant under equality considerations. Supporters argue that affirmative action measures are not used in an arbitrary way, but with the aim of redressing a situation of severe disadvantage due to societal or past discrimination. [60] It is clear that decisions with regard to the scope and type of affirmative action measures, the mix of incentives and deterrents, and implementation modalities, including "phasing out" procedures, need to be carefully examined and agreed upon in a participatory manner. Affirmative action measures are necessary to put everyone on an equal footing, especially when socio-economic inequalities between groups are profound and arise out of a history of oppression and social exclusion of one group by the other.

The importance of gathering the right data

Broadening the knowledge base on discrimination at work

208. A key condition for effectively tackling discrimination at work is to know its extent and nature. Data collection is necessary to broaden the knowledge base on discrimination, to guide policy choices, to assist in the design, implementation, monitoring and evaluation of policy interventions, and to set targets and benchmarks to measure progress towards equality. Ascertaining the magnitude of discrimination at work is a challenging task, owing to conceptual limitations and also to inadequacies in the collection of relevant data. Some inequality measurements are often used as a proxy to show the existence of discrimination. Some significant progress has been made with regard to the measurement of gender inequalities but much work remains to be done for gender and for other grounds of discrimination.

Technical and financial considerations

209. The format or structure of readily available data (e.g. census, household surveys, establishment surveys) might not yield information that allows a direct link with discrimination to be established. Complementary information is required, or proxies for this information selected. Efforts have been devoted to the methodology of producing labour statistics [61] and budgets [62] with regard to discrimination on the basis of sex, but the same theoretical and methodo-

---

[59] United Nations Economic and Social Council: *Prevention of discrimination and protection of indigenous peoples and minorities: The concept and practice of affirmative action*, Progress report submitted by M. Bossuyt, Special Rapporteur, in accordance with resolution 1998/5 of the Sub-Commission on the Promotion and Protection of Human Rights, doc. E/CN/.4/Sub.2/2001/15, 26 June 2001.

[60] J. Faundez: *Affirmative action: International perspectives* (Geneva, ILO, 1994), pp. 4-5.

[61] See, for example, A. Mata Greenwood: "Gender issues in labour statistics", in *International Labour Review* (Geneva, ILO), Vol. 138, No. 3, 1999, pp. 273-286.

[62] See D. Budlender and G. Hewitt: *Gender budgets make more cents: Country studies and good practice* (London, Commonwealth Secretariat Publications, 2002). At the fifth Meeting of Commonwealth Ministers Responsible for Women's Affairs, the ministers agreed that the national macro-budgetary process was an appropriate entry point for engendering macroeconomic policies. The Gender Budget Initiative (GBI) was a Commonwealth Secretariat pilot project started in 1995 in Barbados, Fiji, Saint Kitts and Nevis, South Africa and Sri Lanka. Subsequently, this project was developed by the Commonwealth Secretariat, UNIFEM and the International Development Research Centre in Canada into the Gender Responsive Budgets Initiative (GRBI), which has been implemented in 40 countries. See http://www.thecommonwealth.org/gender/index1.htm

logical work has not been carried out in respect of other manifestations of discrimination.

210. Data collection and processing is a costly exercise. In addressing the cost, the trade-off between trying to ensure comprehensiveness and representativeness needs to be taken into account.

Political and ideological orientations

211. Some States are reluctant to collect specific statistics – for example, those related to race – either because they fear that this will undermine social cohesion or because it will expose governments to political pressure. [63] Racial minorities worry that ethnic/racial statistics will be misused to their detriment, and that the gathering of statistics on race or ethnic origin may reinforce negative racial stereotypes. [64] Despite these difficulties, many countries have attempted to produce ethnic/birthplace or nationality projections. [65] Problems arise, however, on when and how data are collected and how this should be used.

Concerns about privacy

212. A major concern is the use to be made of the data collected. Many activities performed routinely in the employment context entail the processing of personal data of workers, sometimes data of a very sensitive nature when related to, for example, their health status (HIV/AIDS, disabilities etc.). The 1997 ILO code of practice on protection of workers' personal data sets recommendations and guidelines. Over the past decade, regulations have multiplied to address both individual rights and concerns and commercial interests.

Developing a measuring tool

213. People experiencing discrimination at work suffer from a deficit of economic and social rights. Countries and non-governmental organizations need a handy measure to determine, if not the exact size of the rights gap, at least the direction of the movement and the speed at which it is occurring. Some work-related indicators are readily available and can measure notable dimensions of equality. For example, occupational segregation and pay data, taken together, constitute useful measures of equality. But occupational statistics are not universally available, and calculating segregation goes beyond raw data. It is also clear that measuring inequality will involve more than one dimension, and will require a composite index. One component would certainly have to be labour force participation rates, the first step to equality. A second component might be sectoral employment, where data are available almost universally. Employment status and occupational data, where available, might make up the third and fourth components. Wage or income data should form the final component. This illustrates the possible directions for methodological work towards measuring discrimination and equality. An integrated

---

[63] P. Simon: "La statistique des origines: l'ethnicité et la 'race' dans les recensements aux Etats-Unis, Canada et Grande-Bretagne" ["The statistics of origin: Ethnicity and 'race' in censuses in the United States, Canada and Great Britain"], in *Sociétés Contemporaines* (Paris, IRES-CO), No. 26, 1997, pp. 11-44.

[64] A. Krizsán (ed.): *Ethnic monitoring and data protection: The European context* (Budapest, CEU Press Ltd., 2001). This book focuses on the Roma people in eight European countries.

[65] M. Storkey: "A review of literature on ethnic group projections", in *Population projections by ethnic group: A feasibility study* (London, HMSO, 2002).

framework of decent work indicators is being developed within the Office; some of these indicators reflect direct and indirect discrimination and measure some dimensions of equality. [66]

Education and vocational training help inclusion

Deliberate policy measures

214. Deliberate policy measures aimed at ensuring equal access to, and equal opportunities in, the acquisition and maintenance of educational and skill endowments are crucial to redress inequities in labour market outcomes across social groups. They act as a powerful device to overcome unproductive, volatile, low-paid and low-status work in which groups that are discriminated against are often clustered. [67] From a society's perspective, the benefits derived from more productive and more responsible citizens may surpass private returns.

Significant progress

215. Around the world, significant progress has been made in educational attainment and projections look encouraging, although important regional differences still persist. Almost 80 per cent of the world's population aged 15 years and over is now literate. Women still make up two-thirds of the world's adult illiterates but, in all regions of the world, they are gaining access to education and literacy, and at a faster rate than men. [68] In many countries, there has been a decline in the gender gap in primary and secondary schooling and a significant increase in women's enrolment in higher education compared to men's. Improvements in girls' education, particularly primary education, are the result of the greater emphasis placed by public policy on access to universal primary education compared to access to higher education and skills development. However, an exclusive emphasis on improving girls' access to primary education could jeopardize women's future employment and income opportunities, especially in countries where cheap and low-skilled female labour may cease to constitute a comparative advantage in the global economy.

216. Although higher educational attainment is generally associated with higher earnings, it does not necessarily contribute to reductions in disparities in the labour market. In countries where women have been able to achieve higher levels of education, the effect of more education on the earnings of men and women does not follow a consistent pattern. In some countries, such as the **Netherlands**, **New Zealand** and the **United Kingdom**, earnings differences have narrowed considerably, while in others, such as **Italy** and **Sweden**, they have tended to be particularly high at the tertiary level. [69] Similarly, other discriminated-against groups have not derived returns commensurate to expectations from education.

217. For example, in **Brazil**, a combination of tight budgets and a new schooling population, which was previously excluded from the system and, as a result of this, requires more attention, explain the decrease in returns to

---

[66] R. Anker, I. Chernyshev, P. Egger, F. Mehran and J. Ritter: *Measuring decent work with statistical indicators*, Policy Integration Paper No. 1 (Geneva, ILO, 2002).

[67] Conclusions concerning human resources training and development included in the resolution concerning human resources training and development adopted by the International Labour Conference, 88th Session, Geneva, 2000, available at http://www.ilo.org/public/english/standards/relm/ilc/ilc88/resolutions.htm#III

[68] See the UNESCO Institute of Statistics database for literacy rates by regions and gender, available at http://www.uis.unesco.org. These figures were released to mark International Literacy Day, 8 September 2002.

[69] OECD: *Education policy analysis: Education and skills 2001* (Paris, 2001), p. 80. A similar feature has also been revealed for Latin America, see ILO: *Labour Overview 2002* (Lima, 2002).

education from the end of the 1970s.[70] Another factor that appears to explain unequal returns to education is the degree of inequality or equality prevailing in society.

218. Vocational training, by equipping groups that are discriminated against with the skills needed to improve their productivity and income, can play an important role in broadening and improving employment and income opportunities for these groups.[71] However, vocational training policies and institutions must find and overcome the barriers that members of certain groups may face at different stages of the training process. In least developed countries, where public training institutions are much more important than private training providers, the importance of an inclusive training policy is even more apparent. However, in the past, training has mostly benefited the better-off groups and prepared them for employment in the formal economy. Different forms of direct or indirect discrimination occur in skills development programmes and practice. Gender stereotyping is often found in vocational guidance, and some training schemes even worsen occupational segregation by sex. As regards vocational training, young women are more likely to follow school-based systems, while a higher proportion of young men follow in-house apprenticeship or dual-systems training. Since vocational training is the main entry path into skilled employment, young women's employment opportunities are more limited than those of their male peers.

219. In **Thailand**, prior to the 1997 economic crisis, the skills that women tended to learn in public and private training institutions reproduced gender stereotypes and strengthened sex segregation, through care-based and entry-level service-based courses (e.g. child and elderly care, traditional Thai massage, office assistance and hotel maid services). The aftermath of the 1997 economic crisis has pushed women towards new occupational skills, such as commercial cooking, computers and electronics, where the participation of men and women is more equal.[72]

220. The reforms of the vocational education and training of the 1990s, as in Latin America, for example, have tended to focus on the need to promote enterprise-based training in both the formal and informal economy, to encourage greater private-sector participation, to increase cost recovery and to depend less on public-sector provision. But privatizing this training has proved to be more demanding than originally anticipated. The training needs of small and micro-enterprises, which absorb a large number of members from discriminated-against groups, have been difficult to identify. The demand for training among micro-enterprise operators and workers has remained limited because of their inability to afford the cost that this entails and to articulate their demands effectively. Alternative approaches combining "participatory skill development", with emphasis on agency and local skills and knowledge, and services to help overcome disadvantage and discrimination in spheres other than work have developed (see box 2.2).[73]

Broadening and improving employment and income opportunities

---

[70] A. Rands Barros: "Is the quality of education improving in Brazil? Some empirical tests from a market-based perspective", in R.T. McCutcheon and F.L.M. Taylor Parkins (eds.): *Work 2001: First international conference on employment creation in development: Conference proceedings 2-5 April 2001, University of Witwatersrand, Johannesburg, South Africa*.

[71] P. Bennell: *Learning to change: Skills development among the economically vulnerable and socially excluded in developing countries*, Employment and Training Paper No. 43 (Geneva, ILO, 1999).

[72] B. Suriyasarn and B.P. Resurrection: *Action research: Gender dimension of skills development in vocational training in Thailand* (Bangkok, ILO and Ministry of Labour and Social Welfare, 2002).

[73] P. Bennell, op. cit.

Box 2.2

Strengthening technical and vocational training of low-income women in Latin America (FORMUJER)

Building on the achievements of a programme on the promotion of women's participation in vocational and technical training implemented in the early 1990s,[1] the ILO Inter-American Research and Documentation Centre on Vocational Training (CINTERFOR), with the support of the Inter-American Development Bank, started in 1998 a programme to strengthen technical and vocational training of low-income women (FORMUJER) in Argentina, Bolivia and Costa Rica. Acting simultaneously on the logic of gender mainstreaming in vocational training system strategies and adopting specific measures focusing on women in unfavourable conditions, the programme aims to enable women to:

— learn non-traditional competencies (competencies diversification);

— access new niches of employment (creation of new competencies);

— reassess the value of old competencies historically performed by women with a view to promoting innovation and marketing new niches of employment.

As part of the materials and methodologies that FORMUJER is developing, training modules for employability and citizenship have been realized. These modules are meant to serve as a "tool box" for the Latin American vocational training system to reinforce and to improve its gender relevance and equity.

The education of citizens, both men and women, converges nowadays with the training of men and women workers. In both cases, individuals must act in the three fundamental dimensions of life's development, namely: in relationship with themselves, in relationship with others (family life and partaking of the broader social scene) and in relationship with their surrounding environment. Consequently, developing people's employability and educating them for responsible citizenship are complementary processes. This is an example of going beyond the workplace to promote gender equality and, at the same time, using the workplace as an entry point to promote equality in other spheres of society.

[1] CINTERFOR: *Training for decent work* (Montevideo, ILO, 2001), p. 36.
Source: http://www.ilo.org/public/english/region/ampro/cinterfor/temas/gender/formujer/index.htm
and http://www.ilo.org/public/english/region/ampro/cinterfor/temas/gender/doc/modul.htm

---

Promoting more equitable labour outcomes

221. As part of a comprehensive equal opportunity programme, education and training policy can promote more equitable labour market outcomes. The trend towards lifelong learning, which rejects a society structured on the basis of age in which education and training are one-off undertakings experienced early in life, is an effective device to prevent discrimination against older workers.

222. While individual human capital endowment is important, the demand for a worker's labour depends on the broader economic environment. When the labour market is tight, it is easier for disadvantaged people to find jobs, but, when the labour market is slacker, factors other than qualifications, such as employers' preferences and personal networks, gain more weight. Therefore, supply-side measures of education and training are important, but need to be supported by other more active equality-enhancing measures in the labour market.

The role of employment services

The role of employment services

223. Employment services have a role to play in matching supply and demand in the labour market. Through their role as gatekeepers they can be both perpetrators of discriminatory practices in the labour market and pro-

moters of equal opportunities in access to work and improved transparency in the labour market.

224. In a world in which powerful demographic forces are creating an ageing labour force in developed countries and continuing population growth in most developing countries is creating problems of youth unemployment, employment services will continue to be heavily involved in assisting people who are disadvantaged in the labour market.

225. The current shifts towards privatization have brought to an end the monopoly of public employment services. Both public and private employment agencies need to find a balance of cooperation, complementarity and competition in promoting equal opportunities in access to work in performing their functions, such as job-broking, providing labour market information, administering labour market adjustment programmes and administering unemployment benefits. [74]

Finding a balance

226. The Private Employment Agencies Convention, 1997 (No. 181), and its accompanying Recommendation (No. 188), set out the principle of non-discrimination in the way private employer agencies treat workers and draw up and publish vacancy notices or offers of employment. These instruments encourage private employment agencies to promote equality in employment through affirmative action programmes. [75]

227. An example of the positive role that employment services can play in promoting equal opportunities is the set of facilitating policies and measures adopted by the Shanghai Municipal Government in **China** on employment services. This included extending training opportunities to employers and employees in the informal economy, among which was the "4050" project. This project targeted laid-off workers aged over 40 for women and over 50 for men, who encountered difficulties in re-employment because of societal attitudes towards age. [76]

Balancing work and family

228. Over the past ten years, women's participation in the labour market has increased markedly in almost all regions of the world, although with varying degrees. Among OECD countries in 2000, the female labour participation rate was highest in the Nordic countries and lowest in **Italy**, **Mexico** and **Turkey** (see Annex 3, table 1).

229. At the same time, the proportion of smaller households headed by single parents has grown in almost all OECD countries. The majority of single parents comprise women, and their employment rate has risen sharply. The proportion of female-headed households has also increased in many developing countries. Despite the redistribution of financial responsibility within the family, the burden of household duties and care functions still continues to fall largely on women's shoulders, [77] thus reflecting the endurance of well-entrenched assumptions about work, family, society and gender roles in these spheres. [78] For a long time, tasks pertaining to the "care" domain were

Well-entrenched assumptions

---

[74] P. Thuy, E. Hansen and D. Price: *The public employment service in a changing labour market* (Geneva, ILO, 2001), pp. xv-xxi.

[75] Article 5 of Convention No. 181 and Paragraphs 9 and 10 of Recommendation No. 188.

[76] J. Howell: *Good practice study in Shanghai on employment services for the informal economy* (Geneva, ILO, 2002), pp. v, 14 and 15.

[77] C. Sirianni and C. Negrey: "Working time as gendered time", in *Feminist Economics* (London, Routledge Taylor and Francis Group), Vol. 6, No. 1, Mar. 2000, pp. 59-76.

[78] R.C. Barnett: "A new work-life model for the twenty-first century", in *Annals of the American Academy of Political and Social Science*, Vol. 562, Mar. 1999, pp. 143-158.

considered a private matter to be addressed through private arrangements in the household. More recently, the question of how to balance work and family has gained recognition as an appropriate topic for state intervention. There is growing consensus on the need for a more balanced division of responsibility between the State, enterprises, communities, families and individuals.

Why is it important to get the work/family balance right?

230. In the present context of plummeting fertility rates, rises in life expectancy and restrictive immigration policies in many European countries, it is crucial to keep working mothers in the workforce to compensate for shortfalls in labour supply and for the payment of the taxes needed to finance welfare provision for the aged and those in poor health (see box 2.3).

Work/family policies

231. Work/family policies also help maintain women's labour market skills by avoiding forced work breaks during child-rearing years. This translates into women's greater productivity, due to investments in firm-specific experience and training.[79] In turn, this improves their career development prospects, employability and earning rates in the long run.

Box 2.3

Highlights and impact of a study on the costs and benefits of childcare in Zurich, Switzerland

In 2000, the Social Department of the City of Zurich launched a study on the costs and benefits of childcare with the aim of redressing the severe imbalance between the supply of childcare facilities and the size of the eligible population in Zurich (and elsewhere in Switzerland).

Main findings

Socialization of children: More and more children grow up as an only child. Childcare centres allow social interaction and social learning that facilitate transition to school.

Loss of human capital of parents: Women's educational achievements are today as high as men's. Women's withdrawal from the labour market translates into a waste of educational investment and lower remuneration and lower social security throughout and after their working life.

Benefits for tax payers and poverty reduction: Availability of good quality and affordable childcare, by retaining parents in the labour market, reduces the number of households living in poverty, thus benefiting tax payers in the form of social benefits savings.

Qualified employees for firms: Inability to retain qualified young parents entails significant costs to firms in terms of losses in know-how, recruitment costs and training costs, among others.

Main outcomes/impacts

Increased public subsidies for childcare: In 2002, the annual contribution to childcare was raised from 19 million to 25 million Swiss francs in Zurich. About 200 million Swiss francs were allocated over four years by the federal Government for the creation of new childcare centres countrywide.

Source: K. Muller and T. Bauer: Kindertagesstätten zahlen sich aus, Edition Sozialpolitik, Nr. 5a, Sozialdepartement der Stadt Zurich (The importance of day-nurseries, Social Policies Publication, No. 5a, Department of Social Affairs of the City of Zurich) (Zurich, 2001). Available at: http://www.stadt-zuerich.ch/kap10/kindertagesstaetten

---

[79] Y. van der Meulen Rodgers: *Protecting women and promoting equality in the labour market*, op. cit.

Fiscal measures

232. Decisions of partners about entering, remaining in or quitting the labour market depend, to a considerable extent, on taxation policies. Taxation systems can be joint or separate. In joint systems, the partner earning the lower income faces higher marginal tax rates in a progressive taxation system. Conversely, a separate taxation system raises the incentive for the partner with lower earnings to enhance his or her income, through employment continuity. Over the past 30 years, most OECD countries have shifted from a joint to a separate taxation system.[80] In other instances, the preferred option has been to grant workers tax relief measures, providing deductions for the costs associated with childcare or care for another dependent family member.

Shortening work schedules

233. One way of allowing working parents to harmonize work and family is by permitting them to work fewer hours than a full-time week or by modifying their hours of work according to their care responsibilities. One of the most common forms of working time flexibility in the majority of OECD countries is part-time work (see Part II, Chapter 1, figure 3).

234. Part-time work has permitted working mothers to reconcile domestic duties with remunerated work and has allowed employers to adjust with greater flexibility to market fluctuations. As has already been emphasized in Part II, Chapter 1, part-time work also has its drawbacks. Working conditions are generally significantly worse than those of equivalent full-time workers[81] and difficulties in moving from part-time work to full-time work are significant.

Care services for children and other dependent family members

235. Care services to help working parents, particularly women, reconcile their family and child-rearing responsibilities with remunerated employment are another crucial device to achieve gender equality and social equity. Childcare arrangements vary in terms of the forms they can take, the actors involved and the sharing of the relevant financial costs. Differences are linked to the general cultural perceptions of, and attitudes towards, the family.[82]

236. In the **United Kingdom** and the **United States**, childcare is viewed as an individual responsibility. This raises problems of social equity, as low-income and single-parent families tend to experience greater difficulties in gaining access to high-quality childcare. In Continental Europe, where the scope for government intervention is larger, childcare arrangements still remain heavily family-based, with some exceptions. In **Argentina**, **Brazil** and **Chile**, employers, depending on the number of female employees, must shoulder fully childcare expenses, but enforcement of this is lax. The provision of adequate minding facilities for dependent family members other than children is equally indispensable. In developing countries, where the scale of the HIV/AIDS pandemic is dramatic, the absence of adequate care structures has compelled many parents to rely on their children, usually girls, to provide this care with enormous costs to them in terms of lost schooling and lower future earnings.

---

[80] OECD: *Employment Outlook 2001*, op. cit.

[81] OECD: *Employment Outlook 1998* (Paris, 1998).

[82] J. Plantenga and J. Hansen: "Assessing equal opportunities in the European Union", in M. Loutfi (ed.): *Women, gender and work* (Geneva, ILO, 2001), pp. 273-304.

Maternity protection and parental leave

237. Maternity protection is concerned with the protection of the health of mothers, as return to work is subject to their physical readiness for work, and provides them with time-off for child-bearing. It is a prerequisite for women's full participation in the labour force and, hence, a pillar of equal opportunity policies for women at work. In Latin America, maternity benefits are compulsory and covered by the social security system or general taxation. Enforcement, however, is uneven and non-compliance appears to be related also to women workers' ignorance of their maternity leave entitlements.

238. Maternity leave is paid in all European countries, although the amount that women on maternity leave receive and the period for which they are paid differ greatly across the region. In the **United States**, maternity leave is unpaid and eligibility is linked to length of employment, hours of work and the size of the enterprise. Some companies, nonetheless, have provided a period of leave – either paid or unpaid – to their employees, usually the more skilled and productive women, showing the value attached to higher levels of firm-specific tenure and overall work experience.[83] In the Middle East and North Africa, the generous maternity protection benefits provided by the public sector and the perceived "respectability" of this type of employment, explain the appeal that it has traditionally had for women. Private employers' concern about maternity protection costs is deemed to account for the low share of female labour in the private sector.[84]

239. Parental leave can be taken by either the mother or the father and consists of prolonged periods of absence from work. It does not entail loss of employment or loss of any associated entitlements and can be used only by workers with young children.[85] Reliance on parental leave depends on the scope of coverage, the period of time available for leave and whether the leave is paid or unpaid. In the **United States**, where parental leave is unpaid, 63.9 per cent of workers with family responsibilities and in need of taking time off did not do so because they could not afford it. In many European countries paternal leave is paid mostly through public funding. However, the proportion of eligible fathers taking advantage of this measure is still very low. Fear of discrimination when it comes to future income and career prospects and of being ridiculed by co-workers explain in part this situation.

Family-friendly arrangements promoted by enterprises

240. Family-friendly workplaces tend to be more "popular" in large companies that are capital-intensive than in small or medium-sized establishments characterized by, or perceived as being of, low productivity. These include the retail and other service industries or sectors where productivity is hard to measure. Even in enterprises with work/family arrangements, not all employees have equal access to them. Skill levels, high job tenure or investment in training are determinants of eligibility.[86] According to the limited evidence available, the incidence of family-friendly practices among small and large enterprises is very similar and neither type of business considers work/

---

[83] J. Waldfogel: "Family leave coverage", in *Monthly Labor Review* (Washington, DC, United States Department of Labor), Vol. 122, No. 10, 1999, pp. 13-21.

[84] CAWTAR, UNDP and AGFUND: *Globalization and gender: Economic participation of Arab women* (Tunis, Centre of Arab Women for Training and Research (CAWTAR), 2002).

[85] P. Bollé: "Parental leave", in M. Loutfi (ed.): *Women, gender and work*, op. cit., pp. 347-367.

[86] M. Gray and J. Tudball: *Family-friendly work practices: Differences within and between workplaces*, Australian Institute of Family Studies Research Report No. 7 (Melbourne, 2002).

family reconciliation measures a priority.[87] Work/family arrangements and benefits tend to be less formal in small enterprises that in larger businesses. However, work/family problems appear to be fewer in small enterprises because of less social distancing of employees from the business owner and greater pressure from co-workers.[88]

241. Reconciling work with a satisfying family or personal life is a pressing challenge of modern living. There is a danger that work/family policies, which are often aimed explicitly or implicitly at women in particular, may end up reinforcing the image of women as "secondary earners" and accruing to the double burden of working women. It is important to identify which work/family balancing arrangements are more conducive to overcoming discrimination against women and achieving equal opportunities in the labour market for both women and men.

---

[87] S.M. MacDermid, L.C. Litchfield and M. Pitt-Catsouphes: "Organizational size and work-family issues", in *Annals of the American Academy of Political and Social Science*, Vol. 562, Mar. 1999, pp. 111-126.
[88] V. Perotin, A. Robinson and J. Loundes: *Equal opportunities practices and performance in small and medium-sized enterprises: Preliminary findings* (Geneva, ILO, 2002).

Part III. The ILO and the social partners in action

1. The ILO: A long history of combating discrimination at work

242. ILO action to eliminate discrimination and promote equality in the world of work is wide-ranging, resulting in valuable experience. This overview provides illustrations of the many ILO initiatives in this domain, to indicate the range of approaches and means of action developed by the Organization over the years. Work in this area has been spread across several technical departments and units. This chapter does not refer to the specific initiatives of the Bureaux for Employers' and Workers Activities. These are dealt with in Part III, Chapter 2, which focuses on employers' and workers' organizations and enterprises.

ILO action is rooted in the international labour standards

243. The principle of the elimination of discrimination in respect of employment and occupation is a distinct feature of ILO standard setting and permeates much of the ILO's technical cooperation activities. This principle has been promoted through ILO standards in different ways. Some Conventions and Recommendations, such as fundamental Conventions Nos. 100 and 111, aim specifically at promoting equality and eliminating discrimination; others, such as the Employment Policy Convention, 1964 (No. 122), and the Human Resources Development Convention, 1975 (No. 142), address this question through specific provisions. And yet other instruments focus on distinct categories of workers, such as the Rural Workers' Organisations Convention, 1975 (No. 141). This variety of international labour standards confirms that no single policy instrument suffices to address all discrimination in employment and occupation and, consequently, a combination of policies is required.

A variety of international labour standards

244. Assistance in drafting and implementing labour legislation that bans discrimination and promotes equality at the national level is one of the pillars of ILO action in this field. The ILO supervisory system continues to play an important role in ensuring that national law, policies and practice are consistent with the principles, rights and responsibilities laid down in ratified Conventions. Advisory services and technical cooperation have been carried out to allow ratification or they have originated as a response to the comments of the Committee of Experts on the Application of Conventions and Recommendations.

Labour legislation   245. The development of manuals and other tools to ensure that labour law
guidelines   drafting is consistent with the principle of non-discrimination constitutes an
integral part of this effort, as illustrated by the *Labour Legislation Guidelines*.[1]
These guidelines provide practical approaches to the promotion of the fundamental principles and rights at work, including the elimination of discrimination, through labour legislation. Recognizing their key role in enforcing labour
law, the ILO has carried out training activities on international labour standards for government officials and law-drafters, trade unions and employers' organizations, as well as for judges and legal educators.

The ILO and racial discrimination: Paving the way for institutional change

The ILO in post-apartheid South Africa and Namibia: Building an affirmative action policy

246. In the mid-1990s, following the end of apartheid in **Namibia** and **South
Africa**, the governments of those countries turned to the ILO for technical assistance to revise their legal frameworks in order to eliminate discrimination
in employment. This included policy advice and the provision of comparative
labour law examples and drafting expertise for the elimination of discrimination based on race, sex and disability.

247. In **South Africa**, the 1995 Labour Relations Act contained, under the
Chapter "Unfair Dismissal", a ban on dismissing an employee "on any arbitrary ground, including, but not limited to race, gender, sex, ethnic or social
origin, colour, sexual orientation, age, disability, religion, conscience, belief,
political opinion, culture, language, marital status or family responsibility".[2]
A code of good practice on the handling of sexual harassment cases was subsequently adopted.[3] The enactment of the Employment Equity Act in 1998 was
the culmination of a participatory process with wide stakeholder involvement,
supported by the ILO. This Act prohibits unfair discrimination on a wide range
of grounds,[4] requires designated employers to implement affirmative action
measures for black people, women and people with disabilities and to submit
reports on actions taken. It also establishes a "tripartite-plus" Commission on
Employment Equity, which undertakes research and has an advisory function
to the Minister of Labour, and is authorized to make awards recognizing
achievements of employers in furthering the application of the Act.

248. In **Namibia**, the ILO assisted in the drafting of the Affirmative Action
(Employment) Act adopted in late 1998,[5] and participated in sensitization activities for social partners and other stakeholders (black people, women's
groups and people with disabilities). Extensive training on employment equity
and affirmative action was carried out. ILO assistance also contributed to the
inclusion of workplace issues in the Namibian National Gender Plan of Action
(1998-2003) of the Office of the President. The Namibian legal policy and approaches to combat discrimination on the basis of race and sex and other

---

[1] Accessible on the Internet at http://www.ilo.org/public/english/dialogue/ifpdial/llg/main.htm

[2] South African Labour Relations Act 1995, section 187(1f).

[3] South Africa, General Notice 1367 of 17 July 1998.

[4] The non-exhaustive list includes race, sex, pregnancy, marital status, family responsibility,
ethnic or social origin, colour, sexual orientation, age, disability, religion, HIV status, conscience, belief, political opinion, culture, language and birth (South African Employment
Equity Act, No. 55 of 1998, section 6).

[5] See ILO NATLEX database, available at http://natlex.ilo.org/txt/e98nam01.htm

     TIME FOR EQUALITY AT WORK

forms of discrimination have been models for other countries in the subregion.[6] Technical advice on equality in labour legislation has since been provided to **Botswana** and **Malawi** and is currently being provided to **Zambia** in the context of general labour law revisions.

Brazil: Campaigning for equality in respect of diversity

249. During the 82nd Session of the International Labour Conference, in June 1995, **Brazil** noted the existence of discrimination in the labour market and requested ILO assistance to implement fully Convention No. 111. A technical cooperation project aimed at raising awareness and disseminating information on Convention No. 111 and its implementation began in September 1995, with ILO support.

250. Two institutions were created: the Multidisciplinary Technical Group (GTM), comprising representatives from each technical department of the Ministry of Labour; and the tripartite Working Group for the Elimination of Discrimination in Employment and Occupation (GTEDEO). Seminars and training activities throughout Brazil were organized and a variety of information material was produced. A campaign embracing all the forms of discrimination listed in Convention No. 111 was launched, with special emphasis on gender and race issues.

251. As a result of the project, the Ministry of Labour and Employment instituted the programme Brazil, gender and race – United for equal opportunities, and Centres for the Prevention of Discrimination in Employment and Occupation were established at the state level within the Regional Departments of Labour and Employment. The centres are responsible for the application of the Government's equal opportunity policy at the state level, dealing with discrimination on the basis of sex and other forms of discrimination. Besides engaging in promotional activities, the centres receive and examine complaints of discrimination, which are channelled eventually to the Labour Prosecution Office, if the mediation provided by Regional Departments of Labour and Employment is unsuccessful. The programme has enjoyed the support of the National Human Rights Bureau (SEDH) of the Ministry of Justice, responsible for the Government's anti-discrimination policy. The second phase of the National Action Plan for Human Rights, launched in 2002, endorses a comprehensive approach to discrimination and diversity, providing specific goals focused on employment and occupations.

From a focus on women workers to gender mainstreaming

252. ILO action for the elimination of discrimination based on sex and the promotion of gender equality represents the bulk of the Organization's work in the fight against discrimination. Efforts to address consistently and adequately gender concerns in all aspects of ILO work were reinforced in 1999 and 2000 with the adoption of the Office policy on gender mainstreaming, which consists of two integrated and complementary components. These comprise: (a) targeted interventions, directed at either women or men or both, to narrow existing gaps in gender equality or to overcome the consequences of past discrimination; and (b) the inclusion of a gender perspective in the design

Policy on gender mainstreaming

---

[6] ILO: *Namibia: Affirmative action in employment*, Final Evaluation Report, doc. NAM/96/MO3/NOR (Geneva, 2000).

and implementation of all programmes and projects.[7] Below are selected examples of both types of measures.

Reducing the rights deficit by promoting women workers' rights

Training, information campaigns and capacity building

253. Lack of awareness of international and national law on equal opportunities for women and men is clearly recognized as a constraint to the effective implementation of these laws. The ILO has addressed this rights deficit with interventions based on a combination of training, information campaigns and institutional capacity building.

254. The *Women workers' rights: Modular training package* and the *International labour standards and women workers: Information kit* produced in 1994 are widely used and have been translated into several languages and adapted to different national contexts.[8] The technical cooperation project Training and Information Dissemination on Women Workers' Rights was launched to promote the use and adaptation of this package in nine countries.

255. This resulted in a wide range of initiatives. In **El Salvador**, a guide for labour inspectors was produced, which includes instruments to verify direct and indirect forms of discrimination. In **Egypt**, a media campaign took place with field visits to industrial zones to show the inhuman conditions in which women had to work. As a result, the Ministry of Labour and Manpower launched an inspection campaign. In **Viet Nam**, the project enhanced the collection of sex-disaggregated data. In **India**, efforts were concentrated on campaigning in the local language in the state of Maharashtra. This facilitated a wide outreach to women workers at the grassroots level both in the formal and the informal economies. In **Hungary**, the project succeeded in placing women workers' rights on the agenda of trade unions, governmental institutions and NGOs. The project contributed to the institutionalization of gender equality, thus increasing ownership and sustainability of the relevant national efforts for the promotion of gender equality. This was also the case in **El Salvador**, **Hungary**, **Mali** and **Suriname**.[9]

256. Since 1995, about 500 representatives from governments and workers' and employers' organizations, as well as representatives of NGOs, lawyers and judges have participated in training activities on women workers' rights organized by the ILO International Training Centre.

More and better jobs for women

257. As an ILO follow-up to the Beijing Platform for Action, the International Programme on More and Better Jobs for Women was started in 1996. This technical cooperation programme assists governments in the implementation of National Plans of Action for More and Better Jobs for Women as part of broader national gender equality initiatives. Distinct features of these national action plans are: (i) their participatory approach in determining priorities and strategies; (ii) their rights-based focus, as awareness raising, legal literacy training and employment creation efforts underscore the fundamental prin-

---

[7] *Gender equality and mainstreaming in the International Labour Office*, Director-General's Announcements, Circular No. 564 (December 1999); and *ILO Action Plan on Gender Equality and Mainstreaming in the ILO*, Governing Body doc. GB.277/5/2 (March 2000).

[8] A recent example is *Women workers' rights and gender equality: A training and resource kit* developed in English and Thai by the ILO Office in Bangkok. The *Trainers' manual: Women workers' rights and gender equality: Easy steps for workers* was produced in 2001 as part of the kit. The manual and accompanying pictures and games aim to reach out to workers with little or no education.

[9] ILO: *Training and information dissemination on women workers' rights*, Evaluation Report, doc. INT/94/M09/NET (Berlin, 1999).

Box 1.1

Tackling multiple discrimination: The Estonian experience

In Estonia, a two-phase National Plan of Action for More and Better Jobs for Women has been in operation since 1999. Extensive capacity building and gender sensitization of policy-makers have taken place.

Valga, one of the poorest counties of Estonia, was selected as the area for a targeted pilot intervention. Rural tourism and alternative agricultural production were identified as sectors with the greatest potential in the area. Over 400 women were trained and provided with support structures and facilities to establish and operate viable business. During the first phase of the action plan, two main concerns emerged: the integration of ethnic Russian-speaking groups into project activities and the age discrimination faced by older women workers. The second phase of the programme seeks to enhance the access of older women workers to employment opportunities through lobby group pressure, and to carry out a job redesign audit in a large textile company in Valga and a promotional campaign.

This experience illustrates the importance of tackling, at each and every stage of project development, the multiple forms of discrimination that women face because of their sex and other personal characteristics.

Source: ILO: *Estonia plan of action for more and better jobs for women: Phase II,* Project doc. EST/98/M01/FIN, (Geneva, 2000).

---

ciples and rights at work; (iii) poverty reduction emphasis with target groups selected from among the poorest communities; (iv) a focus on economic viability and sustainability; and (v) win-win messages – demonstrating in practical ways that more and better jobs for women do not benefit only the women themselves, but also their families (see box 1.1).

An enabling environment for women entrepreneurs

258. In both the formal and the informal economies, there are many women entrepreneurs who account for a large number of enterprises that contribute to national economies. To develop and grow, they require business support services. The Women's Entrepreneurship Development and Gender in Enterprises (WEDGE) unit of the InFocus Programme on Boosting Employment through Small Enterprise Development (IFP/SEED) provides support services to women's businesses and advocates for them. Extensive research is underway to identify and document good practices on women's entrepreneurship support programmes, based on a combination of performance criteria and their potential for replication.

Business support services for women entrepreneurs

259. ILO tools for supporting business development services, such as the Start and Improve Your Business (SIYB) programme,[10] have been adapted to incorporate issues related to gender equality and to ensure that they meet the needs of women entrepreneurs. In **Viet Nam**, in association with OXFAM Quebec, the SIYB programme has targeted women entrepreneurs in provincial areas. In **Kazakhstan**, the SIYB programme has reported that 85 per cent of its trainees are women. While acknowledging the success in meeting the needs of women entrepreneurs in that country, the ILO realized that there was also a need to address the special needs of men who have been retrenched from state-owned enterprises and have withdrawn from economic activity.

---

[10] The SIYB programme is a management-training programme with a focus on starting and improving small businesses as a strategy for creating more and better employment in developing economies and economies in transition.

260. The social partners in **China**, the Chinese Enterprise Confederation/ China Enterprise Directors' Association (CEC/CEDA) established, with ILO assistance, a resource centre to support associations of women entrepreneurs. To generate more positive attitudes towards women entrepreneurs, videos showing them as role models are being developed in **Ethiopia**, **Sri Lanka**, the **United Republic of Tanzania** and **Zambia**.

Empowering women through micro-finance programmes

261. Micro-finance programmes can be a valuable means to empower women and alleviate poverty. However, empowerment cannot be assumed to be an automatic outcome of micro-finance programmes. Specific interventions must be an integral part of the planning process of micro-finance programmes.[11] An example of a holistic approach to promote women's empowerment using micro-finance programmes is the ILO Action to Assist Rural Women in **Guinea**, **Niger**, the **United Republic of Tanzania** and **Zimbabwe**, which began in 1989. The focus of the project was the creation of jobs for low-income rural women through organization and leadership-building, and the provision of credit and training. The second phase of the project, which concluded in 1999, proved the effectiveness of this strategy. Women's participation in local decision-making bodies such as village and district councils had increased and women were more inclined to engage in economic activities, which they were not used to performing before or which were thought to be for men only.[12]

Breaking through the glass ceiling

262. The "glass ceiling", a barrier beyond which women find it difficult to progress in decision-making and managerial positions, is a reflection of social and economic gender discrimination. A tripartite meeting on the topic in the financial and professional services sectors, held in Geneva in 1997, requested the ILO to intensify education programmes focusing on employment, recruitment, career planning, respect for workers' fundamental rights and promotion of women in management.[13] The ensuing research attracted considerable attention from the media as well as from the constituents.[14]

Sexual harassment

Sexual harassment is detrimental to well-being and productivity

263. As far back as 1985, the International Labour Conference recognized that sexual harassment in the workplace was detrimental to employees' well-being and productivity and to their employment and promotion prospects. It called for the inclusion of measures to combat and prevent such harassment in national policies for the advancement of gender equality. To be successful, sexual harassment policies and procedures should include a policy statement, a complaint procedure adapted to sexual harassment that maintains confidentiality, progressive disciplinary rules, and a training and communication strategy. Protection from retaliation must be a key element of any complaint

---

[11] L. Mayoux: *Micro-finance and the empowerment of women – A review of key issues*, Working paper No. 23 (Geneva, ILO, 2000), pp. 5-6.

[12] ILO: *Action to assist rural women: Lessons from Africa*, Case studies of four projects in Zimbabwe, the United Republic of Tanzania, Niger and Guinea (Geneva, 1995), p. iii; and ILO: *Action to assist rural women*, Report of the Final Evaluation Workshop, 13-16 December 1999 in Mefinga, United Republic of Tanzania (Geneva), pp.48-50.

[13] ILO: *Note on the proceedings: Tripartite Meeting on Breaking through the Glass Ceiling: Women in Management*, 15-19 December 1997, Governing Body doc. GB.271/STM/4, p. 35.

[14] L. Wirth: *Breaking through the glass ceiling: Women in management* (Geneva, ILO, 2001).

procedure.[15] So far, ILO activity in this area has primarily focused on research, legislative drafting, training and awareness-raising seminars, especially in Asia and the Caribbean. More work is needed to broaden geographical coverage and to develop technical cooperation activities in order better to equip constituents with instruments to tackle this form of discrimination.

Tackling gender inequalities in remuneration

264. Equal remuneration for work of equal value is integral to the fundamental principle of the elimination of discrimination in employment and occupation and has been a concern of the ILO since its founding. Following the adoption of Convention No. 100, the ILO published, in 1960, an introduction to job evaluation in recognition of the fact that this technique was a key tool in comparing jobs and pay. This was revised in 1986, and a book on equal pay approaches in industrialized countries appeared in 1993.[16] Pilot technical cooperation activities in this area were carried out both at national level and at the level of large public sector undertakings, during the period from the 1970s to the early 1990s. These activities were carried out within the overall framework of national wage policy reform, in recognition of the fact that equal pay matters needed to be addressed within a broader policy framework.

Equal remuneration is integral to the elimination of discrimination

265. ILO technical assistance in ensuring compliance of national law and practice with the provisions of Convention on No. 100 has grown.[17] There have been some notable recent activities. In **Cyprus**, the ILO promoted understanding of the principle through advocacy and training and development of legislation on equal pay and equality guidelines. These efforts led to the establishment of an Equal Remuneration Committee in the labour inspection units that cover employment, and to the adoption of an equal pay act. For many years, the ILO has been providing assistance to the Government of **Mauritius** to redress inequalities in pay between men and women in a number of economic sectors. More recently, on the basis of an assessment of the national situation concerning equal remuneration and equality, the Office provided technical guidance and assistance in re-writing wage regulations, preparing revised job classifications and preparing a Gender Equality Act. Assistance and practical guidance in the implementation of equal remuneration between men and women has been carried out in recent years in **Barbados, Brazil, Cyprus, Czech Republic, Dominica, Estonia, India, Thailand** and **Zimbabwe.**

266. In **Mali**, following a study and a tripartite workshop on the gender pay gap in the formal and private sectors, a two-stage national plan of action to promote equal remuneration for men and women was adopted. This plan aims to extend the survey of equal remuneration to the rural and informal economies.[18] The **Mali** experience confirms the importance of data to initiate any meaningful action, but also that the paucity of data cannot be used as a justification for inaction. The increased awareness of constituents regarding the importance of equality in remuneration has generated consensus on the need to enlarge the

---

[15] N. Haspels, Z.M. Kasim, C. Thomas and D. McCann: *Action against sexual harassment at work in Asia and the Pacific* (Bangkok, ILO, 2001); and A. Reinhart: *Sexual Harassment: Addressing sexual harassment in the workplace: A management information booklet* (Geneva, ILO, 1999).

[16] ILO: *Job evaluation* (Geneva, 1986); and F. Eyraud et al.: *Equal pay protection in industrialized market economies: In search of greater effectiveness* (Geneva, ILO, 1993).

[17] In recent years technical assistance and advisory services have been provided to countries such as Cyprus, Czech Republic, Estonia, Hong Kong, China, India, Pakistan and Thailand (Governing Body docs. GB.277/LILS/6, p. 2, GB.280/LILS/7, p. 2 and GB.283/LILS/8, p. 4).

[18] D. Meurs: *Egalité de rémunération au Mali* [Equal remuneration in Mali] (Geneva, ILO, 2001), p. 33.

scope of actions for its promotion. Cooperating with the social partners at national and international levels is key in this area (see Part III, Chapter 2).

The trafficking of human beings

Child labour and exploitation of migrant workers

267. The trafficking of human beings, a phenomenon that affects mainly women and children, has been a growing concern of the ILO. Trafficking involves the worst forms of child labour and the worst forms of exploitation of migrant workers. It constitutes another manifestation of the severe discrimination that women still confront in many countries. The World Conference against Racism, Racial Discrimination, Xenophobia and Related Intolerance, held in Durban, highlighted that people who are vulnerable to racial and gender discrimination are often victims of trafficking.

268. Through its International Programme on the Elimination of Child Labour (IPEC), the ILO has approached the phenomenon from a preventive angle, by seeking to provide decent work to women in sending countries. In the Mekong subregion, the ILO is supporting a project to combat trafficking in women and children by empowering families, in particular female family members, to take greater control of their lives.[19] Addressing the "demand side" of the trafficking equation remains a major challenge. Further efforts are needed to build a more solid knowledge base in this area together with a broader array of lessons learned in preventing trafficking.[20]

269. In South Asia, the ILO supports a project that promotes a new approach to the rehabilitation of young survivors of trafficking. This approach consists of strengthening the young women's own capacity to overcome the trauma of trafficking. It also mobilizes and empowers, in sending areas, mothers of vulnerable families as a means to prevent trafficking.[21]

Special Action Programme to Combat Forced Labour

270. Further to the discussion of the 2001 Global Report *Stopping forced labour,* a Special Action Programme to Combat Forced Labour was set up under the InFocus Programme on Promoting the Declaration. This action programme is developing a comprehensive prevention approach that places trafficking within the broader economic framework of employment and migration pressures, while taking into consideration the needs of women and children as the primary victims of trafficking. It complements the work of IPEC, which concentrates on the phenomenon of trafficking for purposes of child labour.

Decent work for "invisible" workers: Homeworkers

271. Home work has not been recognized as a distinct form of employment in most countries. Homeworkers are hence "invisible" for the purpose of national statistics. Homeworkers, the majority of whom are low-income and low-skilled women who need to reconcile family responsibilities and domestic chores with income-earning activities, receive little and irregular pay, no social insurance benefits and are seldom organized.[22]

---

[19] The countries involved in the project are Cambodia, China, Lao People's Democratic Republic, Thailand and Viet Nam.

[20] ILO: *The ILO-IPEC Greater Mekong sub-regional project to combat trafficking in children and women,* Project Mid-term Evaluation Report: (ILO, 2002), pp. 5-6.

[21] The South Asia Sub-regional Programme to Combat Trafficking in Children for Exploitative Employment (TICSA) covered Bangladesh, Nepal and Sri Lanka during phase 1 (2000-2002). In phase 2 (2002-2005), the geographical coverage of the project was broadened so as to include also Indonesia, Pakistan and Thailand. For evaluation of phase 1, see J. Kane: *South Asia Sub-regional Programme to Combat Trafficking in Children for Exploitative Employment (TICSA): Evaluation of phase 1* (Geneva, ILO, 2002).

[22] M. Tomei. *Home work in selected Latin American countries: A comparative overview* (Geneva, ILO, 2000), pp. 38-39.

272. The ILO interregional programme *Homeworkers in the Global Economy* has been trying, in Asia, to reduce these decent work deficits. As a result, in **Thailand**, the Office of Homeworkers was set up in the Ministry of Labour and Social Welfare and a policy to promote and protect homeworkers was included in the Eighth National Economic and Social Development Plan (1997-2001). The National Network for Home-based Workers has been created in the **Philippines** (PATAMBA), and a network of homeworkers called Chiangmai Homenet has been established in **Thailand.** These pilot experiences help to render this category of workers more visible. However, further data and research are needed for a better grasp of the magnitude and characteristics of home work, and to address the problems of homeworkers.[23]

Gender mainstreaming and the gender audit

273. The development of tools aimed at strengthening both the ILO's capacity and that of its constituents to address adequately the gender dimensions of social and employment policies is an important component of ILO efforts to promote gender mainstreaming and gender equality (see box 1.2).

274. The ILO has recently concluded the first phase of an Office-wide gender audit, the first of its kind in the United Nations system. The audit aims to promote organizational learning on how to implement gender mainstreaming effectively in the policies, programmes and structures of the Office. It will also help to assess the extent to which ILO policy on gender mainstreaming is being institutionalized. The gender audit used a participatory and self-assessment approach that involved 15 ILO work units implementing ILO programmes in Geneva and the regions. Over 100 men and women from among the constituents, implementing partners and women's NGOs also participated in the field audits, expressing their views on the relevance and adequacy of ILO work on gender.

The gender audit

275. The gender audit pointed to the need to strengthen a collective and systematic process of gender analysis, identified a number of good practices in gender mainstreaming, and facilitated a discussion on wider substantive and operational issues. Recommendations for future work of the ILO in this field included broadening the understanding that gender discrimination is not only an issue in its own right but that it also cuts across all other forms of discrimination, developing the male side of gender analysis, as, for example, in dealing with HIV/AIDS, ensuring the visibility of gender in high profile and interagency frameworks such as the PRSP process, the World Commission on the Social Dimension of Globalization, the Global Employment Agenda and ILO cooperation agreements with countries, and documenting and sharing good practices on gender mainstreaming.

276. The audit pointed out the constraints and gaps that still hinder the implementation of the gender-mainstreaming strategy. Only a minority of ILO documents, including project and programme documents, can be considered to be fully gender mainstreamed. In most of them, gender tends to disappear, has little visibility or is addressed in the background analysis but not reflected in the design of objectives, activities and indicators. Gender concerns have to be *explicit*, the gender perspective *visible* and achievements on gender equality *measurable*. This suggests that monitoring tools are essential to assess how, and to what extent, gender is effectively mainstreamed.[24]

---

[23] The Home Work Convention, 1996 (No. 177), can be a reference instrument in this respect. Article 4 of the Convention refers to equality of treatment and protection against discrimination in employment and occupation.

[24] ILO: *ILO Gender Audit 2001-2002*, Final Report (Geneva, 2002).

Box 1.2

Tools for gender capacity building and mainstreaming

Guidelines for employers on equality at work

These guidelines, prepared by the Bureau for Employers' Activities, lay down some realistic business arguments for developing company action in this area and provide guidance in respect of steps towards the introduction and management of an equal opportunity policy.[1] The guidelines served as a basis for action to promote women in private sector activities through employers' organizations in six countries.[2]

Resource kit for trade unions

To help unions attract and keep women members, the ILO Programme on More and Better Jobs for Women, in collaboration with the Bureau for Workers' Activities and the International Confederation of Free Trade Unions, has produced a modular resource kit on how trade unions can promote gender equality. This resource kit provides background information, practical guidelines and checklists, case studies and examples of good and bad practices for promoting gender equality within the trade union and at the workplace, through collective bargaining, freedom of association and partnerships with other groups in civil society. It shows how trade unions can "share the table and create space" for youths, older workers, workers with disabilities and lesbians and gays.[3]

e.quality@work

e.quality@work is an information base on equal employment opportunites for women and men. It is a compilation of basic information on gender equality laws, policies and programmes that is comprehensive, easy to access, free and open to contributions. It sets out international policy instruments, including relevant international labour standards and national legislation, policies, practices and institutional arrangements in-

troduced by a range of governments, trade unions and public and private sector enterprises. It is available free of charge on CD-ROM and on the Internet.[4]

Open and virtual learning space on Mainstreaming Gender eQuality in the World of Work

The ILO International Training Centre, in collaboration with the Bureau for Gender Equality, developed an online open and distance-learning programme on mainstreaming gender equality in the world of work. The learning space is designed to address the capacity-building needs of ILO staff and constituents to integrate gender equality concerns into their programmes and activities. It is an Internet-based user-friendly tool combining learning modules and existing hypertext media with interactive delivery.

Gender Equality Tool web site

The Gender Equality Tool web site was launched by the ILO on 8 March 2002, International Women's Day.[5] This participatory and database-driven web site is managed by the ILO Bureau for Gender Equality. It is designed to promote information exchange and enhance knowledge on gender-related issues and is accessible in English, French and Spanish. The web site includes sections on gender-related events, resources, links, ILO standards and the ILO Gender Network. As the web site grows, it will cover relevant initiatives and information from ILO offices around the world, as well as from organizations in the United Nations system and academic and research institutes, among others. ILO Gender Network members can directly input information onto the web site, which is one of a growing number of ILO activities aimed at helping to promote gender mainstreaming and gender equality.

[1] ILO: *As one employer to another... What's all this about equality? Guidelines for employers on equality at work* (Geneva, 1996). The guidelines are available at http://www.ilo.org/public/english/dialogue/actemp/download/1998/equal.pdf
[2] Bangladesh, India, Lesotho, Mauritania, Philippines, Swaziland. See ILO: *Promotion of women in private sector activities through employers' organizations,* Progress and Final Evaluation Report doc. INT/95/M03/NOR (Geneva, 1999).
[3] C. Whelton: *Promoting gender equality: A resource kit for trade unions* (Geneva, ILO, 2002).
[4] See http://www.ilo.org/genprom/eeo
[5] See http://www.ilo.org/dyn/gender/gender.home?p–lang=en

Linking poverty and social exclusion to discrimination at work

277. As seen in Part I, Chapter 3, labour market processes are closely associated with poverty, and help to explain the intensity and patterns of poverty and the reasons why poverty tends to be concentrated among particular groups. At the same time, the labour market is an important economic arena through which poverty can be reduced. This is why it is important, within anti-poverty strategies, to tackle discrimination at work occurring on grounds such as race, sex or social origin.

Mainstreaming gender in anti-poverty policies and programmes

278. Research work undertaken on the impact of structural adjustment programmes and on the impact of the Asian crisis on men's and women's levels and forms of employment shows that the elimination of gender-based discrimination at work is a key factor in eradicating poverty. This is the assumption on which the capacity-building Gender, Poverty and Employment (GPE) Programme, the first of its kind in the United Nations system, has been conceived and implemented.[25]

279. The GPE Programme argues that poverty can be traced to employment levels, patterns and inequalities. So, while economic growth is essential and employment creation is strategic to fight poverty, the quality of jobs is just as important. Gender is one major determinant of the quantity and quality of jobs that are made available to women and men. Based on a modular training package, the GPE programme seeks to build national and regional capacities to integrate the gender perspective into the poverty and employment policy agenda. This involves: (a) developing the information and knowledge base of ILO constituents and partners regarding the interfaces of employment, poverty and gender; (b) enhancing dialogue and consensus among social partners and other stakeholders, including representatives of ultimate beneficiaries (e.g. women and men living in poverty) on these issues; and (c) hands-on pilot experience in translating gender-based analysis into practical action.

The Gender, Poverty and Employment Programme

280. The GPE strategy consists of mainstreaming its use, as a tool and resource base, into the relevant ILO technical programmes, while developing distinct and coherent programmes at national and subregional levels. The programme was launched in the countries of the Southern Cone in Latin America, southern Africa, the Arab States and the Commonwealth of Independent States (CIS). Capacity-building activities at the national level are also under way in **Brazil** (see box.1.3).

Box 1.3

Tackling gender and race concerns in fighting against poverty and social exclusion: The experience of Santo André, Brazil

In the framework of the Gender, Poverty and Employment Programme, the ILO contributed to integrating the gender dimension in policies on poverty reduction and the fight against social exclusion adopted by the Municipality of Santo André in Brazil.

Santo André is an economically important municipality of about 800,000 people in the urban area of São Paulo. ILO cooperation with the municipality consisted of supporting gender mainstreaming in public policies. The collaboration with trade unions, academia and NGOs ensured sustainability of ILO action and led to a three-year project aimed at enhancing employment opportunities for women and blacks in the region.

A system of indicators for the follow-up and monitoring of policies on employment and poverty reduction of Santo André was set up. The programme played a key role in integrating gender and race dimensions into the indicators and in the agenda of the Regional Development Agency.

In July 2002, the Municipality of Santo André was awarded the Dubai International Award for Best Practices to Improve the Living Environment for Gender and Citizenship within the Integrated Programme for Social Inclusion.

---

[25] ILO: *Gender, poverty and employment*, op. cit.

Participation in the Poverty Reduction Strategy Paper process: A window of opportunity to promote equality

Decent work – an essential element

281. Decent work is an essential element of sustainable anti-poverty strategies. The participation of the ILO and its constituents in the Poverty Reduction Strategy Paper (PRSP) process provides an excellent opportunity to show the relevance of labour market policies and institutions to combat poverty and promote development. The reason for the ILO's involvement and that of its constituents is "to ensure that employment and other aspects of decent work are addressed as an integral part of the economic and social analyses and policies comprising the initiative"[26]. The ILO is involved in five countries: **Cambodia**, **Honduras**, **Mali**, **Nepal** and the **United Republic of Tanzania.** The strategy is to strengthen the social partners' capacity to get actively involved in the national debate on the PRSP process and policy outcomes. The PRSP process is still in its early stages and all stakeholders are learning from experience. Employment and livelihood opportunities need to be more explicitly addressed in a number of PRSPs. In the **United Republic of Tanzania**, the social partners identified indirect discrimination based on gender and race as a serious and widespread problem in the workplace that needs to be tackled in poverty-elimination strategies.[27]

282. A project recently launched and coordinated by the ILO Bureau for Gender Equality in **China**, **Nepal**, the **United Republic of Tanzania** and **Uganda** will help constituents integrate gender analysis into poverty diagnosis and poverty reduction strategies.[28] To raise the ability of the social partners to influence the PRSP process, country-level capacity building is certainly useful, but it is insufficient. Interventions at the most local level of the PRSP process must be combined with parallel advocacy action at the global level.

Public investment programmes: Promoting inclusive approaches and respect of equality standards

283. The ILO has gained experience in the protection of workers, particularly women, from discriminatory treatment in the framework of publicly funded employment-intensive infrastructure programmes. The ILO Employment-intensive Investment Programme aims to combine economic and social objectives by using public investment in infrastructure and construction as a means to develop labour-intensive, but cost-effective, small and medium-sized enterprises, while simultaneously enforcing labour standards, including those related to equality. This is done through advocacy and training to encourage the use of the tendering and contract system to promote better working conditions and respect for fundamental rights at work, by including relevant provisions in tenders and contracts, and through the provision of advisory services to governments to encourage them to contract enterprises that actually implement labour standards.[29] In **Madagascar**, contractors for rural road rehabil-

---

[26] ILO: Governing Body doc. GB.285/ESP/2, 285th Session, Geneva, November 2002, para. 4.

[27] ILO: *Towards a decent work strategy for poverty reduction in Tanzania*, Social Dialogue Working Paper No. 8 (Geneva, 2002), p. 34.

[28] ILO: *Enhancing the gender mainstreaming capacity of ILO constituents*, Implementation Report INT/02/M67/NET (Geneva, 2002).

[29] See, for example, D. Tajgman and J. de Veen: *Employment-intensive infrastructure programmes: Labour policies and practices* (Geneva, ILO, 1998). The section on wage setting provides guidelines on how to avoid wage systems which discriminate between men and women (p. 63).

itation were encouraged to have at least 25 per cent female employees, a target they managed to reach.

Challenging discriminatory practices through crisis response

284. Crisis response opens a window of opportunity for redressing gender and ethnic economic and social inequalities existing prior to the outbreak of crisis. In a crisis situation, women and men can step out of their socially ascribed roles. Engaging in construction, mechanical and other "male" occupations, acquiring more education while externally displaced, and having no traditional "male" and "female" roles in the absence of men tend to empower women in terms of economic independence, ability as family providers, decision-making and social position. In reconstruction efforts, it is important to involve both men and women to defy perceptions of women's vulnerability and to prevent gender conflict and competition.

Crisis response – a window of opportunity

285. Positive changes in gender roles need and deserve support. Longer-term recovery should capitalize on those changes and avoid returning to pre-crisis, or worse, patterns in order to allow advancement of both women and men and to reduce vulnerability to crises of all concerned. Box 1.4 provides examples of this in **Mozambique** and **Afghanistan.**

286. The challenge ahead is to use crisis response as an entry point to provide a comprehensive framework of interventions that goes beyond activities strictly related to employment promotion and that embraces the decent work paradigm in all its dimensions. This would be more conducive to the achievement of equality in the longer term.

Box 1.4

Positive changes in gender roles in crisis situations

Mozambique: Providing women with the skills needed to rebuild flooded communities in Chokwe

An ILO project was launched to counter the disastrous effects of the 2000 Mozambican floods. It focused on rehabilitating local market-places, providing support for small-animal breeding, training in the use and maintenance of motor-pumps and the manufacture and repair of agricultural tools, and training in sustainable local development and the elaboration of local projects. This gave women, who represented 87 per cent of the beneficiaries, the opportunity to take on new activities and roles.

Afghanistan: Rapid employment-impact pilot programme

In January 2002, the ILO started a rapid employment-impact pilot programme in Afghanistan. One component focuses on women's re-entry into the labour market and aims to provide immediate assistance to female job seekers that have been excluded from the labour market during Taliban rule. Training and retraining activities were organized for women, including professionals (e.g. teachers, doctors, pharmacists and civil servants) to facilitate their rapid reinsertion into their previous occupations.

Source: ILO: *Gender in crisis response factsheet,* available at http://www.ilo.org/public/english/employment/recon/crisis/download/factsheet.pdf

Targeted interventions: A focus on disadvantaged and vulnerable groups

287. There are groups that are in a disadvantaged position in the labour market and that at the same time are vulnerable to exploitation, either because they are poor or because they are vulnerable to becoming poor. To be effective, poverty-oriented labour market policies need to take into account these disadvantages and vulnerabilities. This requires, in some instances, targeting particularly vulnerable subgroups within broadly defined disadvantaged groups.

Promoting indigenous and tribal peoples' rights and livelihoods

ILO influence on national and international policies

288. The ILO has a long history of working on issues relating to indigenous and tribal peoples. As already mentioned, the ILO has adopted the only two international legal instruments on the subject, the Indigenous and Tribal Populations Convention, 1957 (No. 107), and the Indigenous and Tribal Peoples Convention, 1989 (No. 169). Convention No. 169 marked a move from the integrationist and paternalistic approach of its predecessor towards recognition of the value of the culture and institutions of these peoples and their right to be consulted on all decisions affecting their livelihoods. Convention No. 169 refers not only to the rights of these peoples as regards labour and employment, but embraces a broader range of social, economic, civil and political rights. Many of the themes are inextricably linked. It is not possible to eliminate discriminatory practices against indigenous and tribal peoples in the labour market unless issues of education, land rights and other more general social and cultural rights are addressed as well. Convention No.169 has had a great influence on national and international policies on indigenous and tribal peoples, as reflected in the 2002 United Nations Development Programme and Indigenous Peoples: A Policy of Engagement, and the European Council Resolution of 30 November 1998 concerning indigenous peoples within the framework of the development cooperation of the Community and the Member States.

289. The ILO carries out two technical assistance programmes in this area. The Interregional Programme to Support Self-Reliance of Indigenous and Tribal Communities through Cooperatives and Other Self-Help Organizations (INDISCO) was launched in 1993 to improve the socio-economic conditions of indigenous and tribal peoples. It carries out demonstration pilot projects at the grass-roots level and disseminates best practices for policy improvement. A number of lessons can be drawn from these experiences: strengthening institutions of indigenous and tribal communities is necessary for their empowerment, community ownership of development projects is critical for ensuring project sustainability, women's groups emerge stronger and more viable if supported by empowerment processes and if their access to viable and sustainable income generation activities is facilitated.[30] The ILO also carries out its Project to Promote ILO Policy on Indigenous and Tribal Peoples, working mostly at the policy level to promote Convention No. 169, and concentrating on Africa and Asia.

---

[30] ILO: *INDISCO: Support to self-reliance of indigenous and tribal communities through cooperatives and other SHOs*, Tenth progress report 2000 and workplan 2001, doc. INT/93/M07/DAN (Geneva, 2001), pp. 3-4.

290. The lessons learned from the projects feed ILO action at the policy level. In the **Philippines**, INDISCO is assisting the Government, through policy research and national consultations with government institutions and indigenous organizations, in the effective implementation of the Indigenous Peoples' Rights Act of 1997 – a law that was drafted with the technical assistance of the ILO. Activities of the policy promotion project range from support for the development of national policies to the strengthening of indigenous peoples' organizations and indigenous-to-indigenous exchange programmes. In **Kenya**, the ILO project facilitated the informed participation of the country's indigenous peoples in the constitutional review process through an extensive process of nationwide consultations and education process.[31] Work to develop national policies on indigenous peoples is being carried out in **Cambodia**, **Cameroon**, the **Lao People's Democratic Republic**, **Viet Nam** and other countries.

291. In Central America, legal empowerment of indigenous peoples has been pursued under another project through the establishment of national legal teams that were trained and enabled to document and handle specific cases of collective violation of indigenous rights.[32] Despite the ILO being the only organization with international legal standards on the subject matter, work in this area has relied largely on extra-budgetary funding, particularly from the Government of **Denmark** through the Danish International Development Agency (DANIDA).[33]

Addressing discrimination based on disability and HIV/ AIDS status through codes of practice

292. Disability and HIV/AIDS status are widely recognized determinants of disadvantage in the labour market, poverty and social exclusion. Codes of practice have become important devices used by the ILO to prevent and counter discrimination occurring on these two grounds. Codes of practice are non-binding instruments that provide practical guidance on a specific subject, either as a complement to existing Conventions and Recommendations or as the only existing instruments on a particular topic, such as is the case of the ILO code of practice on HIV/AIDS and the world of work.

293. As a co-sponsor of the Joint United Nations Programme on HIV/AIDS (UNAIDS), the ILO raises awareness of the central role of work and the workplace in combating the epidemic and its discrimination aspects. The ILO code of practice on HIV/AIDS and the world of work, adopted in 2001, applies to all workers in the private and public sectors and in the formal and informal economies. It provides guidance on the elimination of stigma and discrimination on the basis of actual or perceived HIV/AIDS status, management and mitigation of the impact of HIV/AIDS, care and support of workers living with HIV/ AIDS or affected by it, and prevention of HIV/AIDS. The code stresses the need to address the gender dimensions of HIV/AIDS, including the male and masculinity perspectives. As part of the ILO's contribution to UNAIDS, training

Combating discrimination based on HIV/AIDS status

---

[31] The new draft Constitution contains many important elements contained in the position paper that represented the collective views of over 15 different indigenous and tribal peoples. Further information and a copy of the position paper can be found on the Kenyan Constitution Review Commission's web site at http://www.kenya. constitution.org

[32] ILO: *Third progress and self-evaluation report: Legal empowerment of indigenous peoples in Central America*, doc. RLA/98/M01/UNF (Costa Rica, 2002), p. 27.

[33] Except for work related to the supervisory mechanisms of Conventions Nos. 107 and 169, which is funded from the regular budget of the ILO.

material has been developed and training courses held. Challenges ahead include setting up a monitoring mechanism to assess the effectiveness of this code of practice and reaching out to workers in the informal economy. Community-based health micro-insurance schemes that cover workers and households that do not have access to statutory systems of social protection security have been another instrument used.[34] Programmes aimed at reducing women's vulnerability to HIV/AIDS, by increasing their economic independence through wider opportunities for self-employment, have also been promoted. It is clear, however, that these initiatives, although useful, are insufficient.

294. In the Caribbean, the social partners have taken the ILO code of practice as a guide for fighting stigma and discrimination based on HIV/AIDS status. The objective to eliminate discrimination has been integrated into the Tripartite Platform for Action on HIV/AIDS and the World of Work in the Caribbean Subregion. The platform contains commitments of governments and employers' and workers' organizations to reduce and eliminate stigma and discrimination based on HIV/AIDS. There is also a project under the new Pan-Caribbean Partnership against HIV/AIDS to identify and remove legal obstacles to eliminating this form of discrimination.[35]

Combating discrimination based on disability

295. The ILO code of practice on managing disability in the workplace is based on the conviction that employers can benefit from employing workers with disabilities, if disability is handled properly. It provides guidance to national authorities, public and private sector employers and employers' and workers' organizations on a range of aspects. These include recruitment and promotion of workers with disabilities, retention of people who acquire a disability and return to work or people who left their job as a result of a disability. The code also stresses that special measures aimed at ensuring equality of opportunity and treatment for workers with disabilities are not to be considered discriminatory against other workers. The challenge is to make the code a useful tool and to develop mechanisms to demonstrate its impact in promoting equality for disabled people.

296. While current efforts seek to strengthen the business case of integrating people with disabilities in the workplace,[36] ILO assistance has traditionally focused on vocational rehabilitation in developing countries, countries in transition and those emerging from armed conflict. For example, the ILO supported the establishment of vocational training and rehabilitation centres in the West Bank and Gaza Strip and in **Bosnia and Herzegovina.** In many developing countries, despite the provision of vocational rehabilitation services and skills training, many disabled people have failed to obtain employment. This is why ILO technical support has been moving towards the provision of assistance to disabled individuals to start up income-generating activities.[37] In **Ethiopia,** a pilot project funded by the Government of **Ireland** seeks to promote the economic empowerment of women with disabilities through entrepreneurship skills development.[38]

---

[34] ILO: *Contributing to the fight against HIV/AIDS within the informal economy: The existing and potential role of decentralized systems of social protection* (Geneva, 2002).

[35] The eight co-sponsors of UNAIDS are UNICEF, UNDP, UNFPA, UNDCP, ILO, UNESCO, WHO and the World Bank.

[36] See, for example, ILO: *Video: Ability Asia* (Bangkok, 2002); and S. Zadek and S. Scott-Parker: *Unlocking potential: The new disability business case* (London, Employers' Forum on Disability, 2001).

[37] ILO: *Vocational rehabilitation and employment of disabled persons*, Report III (1B), International Labour Conference, 86th Session, Geneva, 1998, p. 9.

[38] ILO: *Ireland Aid – ILO Partnership Programme* (Geneva, 2001), p. 3.

297. Vocational training does not automatically ensure that workers with disabilities will gain access to the labour market on an equal footing with other workers, nor do voluntary initiatives by employers guarantee equality of treatment and opportunity for these workers. A range of accompanying measures aimed at creating a discrimination-free environment at work and outside work is necessary.

298. Employment services can contribute to the achievement of such a goal. An ILO project on skills development for the reconstruction and recovery of Kosovo focuses on strengthening the Kosovar public employment offices in the provision of services to their clients, including people with disabilities, demobilized soldiers and ethnic minorities.[39] In contexts where ethnic oppression and discrimination have been severe, employment services' counsellors have an important role to play as mediators and mentors of both the former oppressors and the oppressed. With proper guidance, employment services can play a key role in breaking the cycle of oppression and paving the way for a future society free of ethnic hatred and repression.

Decent treatment of migrant workers

299. With globalization, international migration has intensified and national societies are becoming increasingly diverse. As mentioned earlier, the issue of migrant workers has been placed on the agenda of the 2004 session of the International Labour Conference for general discussion.

International migration intensified

300. Since the early 1990s, the ILO has conducted extensive research on combating discrimination at work against migrant and ethnic minority workers. Many research studies have been published to date, documenting the incidence and characteristics of discrimination in access to employment in various countries. The effectiveness of anti-discrimination training and the impact of legislation have also been examined. Studies have covered **Belgium, Canada, Denmark, Finland, Germany**, the **Netherlands, Spain, Sweden**, the **United Kingdom** and the **United States**; most recently, studies were initiated in **Italy**. Legislation and policy measures inspired by this ILO research were introduced in **Belgium, Denmark** and **Germany**. In a joint initiative with the Council of Europe, a compendium of best practice examples with training material and practitioner guides has been developed.

301. The joint discussion paper produced by the ILO, IOM and OHCHR, in consultation with UNHCR, on international migration, racism, discrimination and xenophobia, which was presented at the World Conference against Racism, Racial Discrimination, Xenophobia and Related Intolerance, held in Durban in 2001,[40] is an illustration of the value of joining forces (see box 1.5). The World Conference in Durban declared unambiguously that racial discrimination against migrant workers was intolerable. ILO standards and experience in combating discrimination in general, and discrimination against migrant workers in particular, and that of its social partners were referred to as key in the Declaration and Programme of Action adopted at the Conference.

---

[39] ILO: *Skills development for the reconstruction and recovery of Kosovo*, Project document (Geneva, 2000).

[40] ILO, IOM and OHCHR, in consultation with UNHCR: *International migration, racism, discrimination and xenophobia*, Discussion paper prepared for the World Conference against Racism, Racial Discrimination, Xenophobia and Related Intolerance (Geneva, 2001).

Box 1.5

Core principles for action against racism and xenophobia faced by migrants

For all migrants, regardless of status:

- Strengthen the rule of law by adoption and implementation in national law of relevant international standards, particularly those recognizing and protecting rights of non-nationals.

- Make racist and xenophobic discrimination, behaviour and action, including against non-nationals and state-less persons, unacceptable and, as appropriate, illegal.

- Elaborate administrative measures, procedures and initiatives to ensure full implementation of legislation, and accountability of all government officials/employees.

- Establish independent national human rights/anti-discrimination monitoring bodies with power to (i) monitor and enforce anti-discrimination legislation; and (ii) receive and act upon individual complaints of discrimination from nationals and non-nationals against both public and private entities.

- Promote respect for diversity and multicultural interaction.

- Encourage political, community and cultural leaders to speak out to promote respect for all, and resolutely to condemn manifestations of racism and xenophobia.

- Encourage communications media to emphasize positive images of diversity and of migration to eliminate negative stereotyping.

- Incorporate multi-cultural and diversity training in educational curricula.

- Mobilize civil society cooperation in promotion, implementation and monitoring of anti-discrimination standards.

Source: ILO, IOM and OHCHR, in consultation with UNHCR: *International migration, racism, discrimination and xenophobia,* Discussion paper prepared for the World Conference against Racism, Racial Discrimination, Xenophobia and Related Intolerance (Geneva, 2001), p. III.

2. Employers' and workers' organizations: Key partners in achieving equality

302. This chapter considers the role and the initiatives of the social partners in addressing discrimination. In a number of cases, the social partners benefited from ILO technical cooperation. These ILO activities are reported here to underline the importance of cooperation with, and action by, employers' and workers' organizations as an essential feature of ILO action.

Voice and representation: Enabling conditions

303. While the State is a key actor in the fight against discrimination and the promotion of equality at work, workers and employers and their representative organizations play an equally important role. No meaningful and lasting outcomes can be attained if employers and workers do not believe in the value and necessity of equality of treatment and opportunities.

304. Two conditions must be met to enable employers and workers to contribute effectively to the elimination of unfair and unjust treatment at work. The first is that workers and employers benefit, *de jure* and *de facto*, from their right to organize into democratic and representative organizations that are able to act without impediments and to engage in effective collective bargaining. Discrimination against workers because of their trade union membership and restrictions on, and violations of, the principles and right of freedom of association are, in fact, widespread.[41] The second is that trade unions and employers' organizations acknowledge the existence of discriminatory practices and combat these practices – starting from within their own institutions. If no deliberate action is taken, trade unions and employers' organizations are destined, like any other social institution, to mirror and sometimes reinforce the sexist, racist or other discriminatory practices prevailing around them.

Two conditions for the elimination of discrimination at work

305. These tasks are hindered by the challenges that the labour movement and employers' organizations are facing because of globalization, the fragmentation of labour markets and the decline in the role of the State in social and

Absence of "voice" mechanisms

---

[41] ILO: *Your voice at work*, Report of the Director-General, International Labour Conference, 88th Session, Geneva, 2000.

economic development.[42] The absence or weakness of "voice" mechanisms and institutions in important sectors of national economies and for a wide spectrum of workers is striking. Agricultural workers, from small farmers to seasonal or casual labour, domestic workers, workers in export processing zones and workers and operators in the informal economy,[43] including illegal migrant workers, are denied freedom of association and the very possibility of exercising their right to the effective recognition of collective bargaining.

306. The barriers that the owners of small and medium-sized enterprises face in securing membership in employers' organizations that represent larger businesses are equally huge. In some instances, this amounts to indirect discrimination towards certain social groups, given the correlation between the size of the enterprises and the owner's sex or national origin. In a situation of dwindling membership of both trade unions and employers' organizations, and the shrinking scope of collective agreements, an equal opportunity agenda can become a window of opportunity.

Trade union efforts to reach out to workers without representation

The needs of a multifaceted labour force

307. In the past two decades, trade unions have recognized the need to organize and represent the interests of an increasingly composite workforce. The heterogeneity of the workforce relates to both the variety of prevalent contractual arrangements and forms of employment, and the diversity of workers' characteristics, such as age, sex and ethnic origin. The motivation for organizing those without representation has not only been to increase membership but also to build wider alliances and to fight for social development. However, catering to the needs of such a multifaceted labour force requires a profound change in trade unions' organizing and alliance-building strategies, their institutional structures and the services that they provide. Levelling the playing field in the world of work means departing from a male, regular and full-time worker model. It requires going beyond the workplace and reaching out to the communities, where unorganized workers live; it demands interventions at both the national and the global levels.

Value chain analysis

308. Value chain analysis has provided valuable insights into how low-income and low-productive producers and low-income countries connect with highly capitalized and large producers and consumers in the global economy.[44] The lower down the chain, the more likely employment relations are to be informal and precarious and the wider the decent work deficits.[45] Using a value chain analytical approach, trade unionists from nine Latin American countries[46] have identified new forms of labour market segmentation, along gender, ethnic/racial and age lines. The difficulty of organizing homeworkers, the "invisible" segment at the lower end of the chain, was acknowledged, but interesting initiatives involving them were revealed. These ranged from support for the creation of homeworkers' organizations (**Chile**) through statutory

---

[42] ILO: *World labour report: Industrial relations, democracy and social stability, 1997-98* (Geneva, 1997).

[43] ILO: *Your voice at work*, op. cit.

[44] R. Kaplinsky: *Spreading the gains from globalisation: What can be learned from the value chain analysis?*, Working Paper No. 110 (Brighton, Institute of Development Studies, 2000).

[45] ILO: *Decent work and the informal economy*, Report VI, International Labour Conference, 90th Session, Geneva, 2002, p. 37.

[46] Brazil, Chile, Colombia, Dominican Republic, Honduras, Mexico, Peru, Uruguay and Venezuela.

reforms to allow social organizations to affiliate (**Colombia**) to pressure for the observance of national laws on home work (**Venezuela**).[47]

309. Declining financial means and the lack of expertise in organizing "non-traditional" workers make the task daunting. Nevertheless, the growth in membership of female workers of minority groups is an indicator that a more socially inclusive strategy pays off. For example in the **United Kingdom**, proportionality and self-organization has translated into higher union membership rates among all ethnic groups, particularly among African-Caribbeans, the only exception being Pakistanis and Bangladeshis.[48] In **Canada**, women's membership in the Canadian Labour Union Congress (CLC) reached 32 per cent in 2000, a rate almost equal to men's membership, which is 34 per cent.[49] A key argument used by the CLC to attract women workers has been that workers who belong to unions earn higher wages than non-unionized workers, and that this is particularly the case for part-time workers, the majority of whom are women. A recent study has found evidence that, in several countries, the impact of unions on women's wages is greater than it is on men's.[50] The limited evidence available also appears to show a positive, although in some instances limited, impact of trade union action on the wages of workers with different ethnic characteristics.

Advantages of more socially inclusive strategies

310. Trade unions have also joined forces regionally to combat racial discrimination. The experience of the Inter-American Trade Union Institute for Racial Equality (INSPIR) is notable. Established in 1996 to devise effective strategies to tackle the widening inequalities between blacks and whites in the labour market, it comprises representatives of the three **Brazilian** national centres (the Single Central Organization of Workers, the General Confederation of Workers and the Força Sindical), the American Federation of Labor and Congress of Industrial Organizations of the **United States** and the ICFTU's Inter-American Regional Organisation of Workers. INSPIR has focused up to now on three main areas of work: research, the development of model clauses to advance racial equality for inclusion in collective agreements, and capacity building for labour leaders and officers to tackle racial questions both politically and at the judicial level.[51]

Employers' associations: Raising the representation of discriminated-against groups

311. Access to membership of, and assistance from, employers' organizations varies between women and men entrepreneurs and according to the size of the enterprise. Business size, in turn, is often linked to the colour or national extraction of the owner. Long-established male-dominated business associations have not always been friendly either to women or to members of minority groups. The creation of women entrepreneurs' associations has often proven an effective device to overcome the greater constraints that women face in the running of their enterprises. These barriers range from more restrictions

Women entrepreneurs' associations

---

[47] ILO: *Trabajo a domicilio y cadenas productivas en América Latina: Desafíos para la acción sindical* [Home work and value chains in Latin America: Challenges for trade union activity] (Geneva, 2002), pp. 13-14.

[48] Information contained in a research project entitled *Handling double disadvantage: Minority ethnic women and trade unions*, from the University of Bristol, Department of Sociology. For further details see http://www.leeds.ac.uk

[49] Canadian Labour Congress: "Canadian Labour Congress wants to double the number of unionized women", in *Unions in Action*, 5 Feb. 2002, available at http://www.icftu.org

[50] T. Aidt and Z. Tzannatos: *Unions and collective bargaining: Economic effects in a global environment* (Washington, DC, World Bank, 2002), pp. 49-50.

[51] ICFTU: *Trade unions say no to racism and xenophobia*, United Nations World Conference against Racism, Racial Discrimination, Xenophobia and Related Intolerance, Durban, 2001, p. 8.

in the selection of the sectors in which women can operate to less access to capital, business support services and the acquisition of experience relevant to entrepreneurship.[52] Another powerful obstacle is the lack of networks and informal support that provide essential sources of information on opportunities, developments and business conditions.

312. Therefore women's needs in respect of entrepreneurship are different from those of men; women's needs also differ among women entrepreneurs themselves and according to the socio-economic contexts, political environments and policy and legal settings in which women entrepreneurs operate.[53] The reasons for women entering into business are similarly diverse. Women in the **United States** or **Canada** may decide to become entrepreneurs in response to the "glass ceiling" problem. In developing countries, compensating for losses in real male wages and providing for the family's survival may often be the principal reason.

Networking and advocacy

313. Networking opportunities are essential to obtain information about new customers and new suppliers. They acquire special relevance for women entrepreneurs, who often find it hard to reconcile time for networking with the other multiple and competing demands on their time. Networking, however, is not enough. In the **United States**, the National Association of Women Business Owners (NAWBO), which has been in existence now for more than 20 years, moved from networking among peers towards a more active engagement in advocacy.[54] This proved essential to bring about changes that were more favourable to women entrepreneurs in bank policies on loans and in government policies on public procurement. The lessons learned through this experience have inspired the work of the Center for International Private Enterprise (CIPE), an affiliate of the United States Chamber of Commerce, which, during the past 13 years, has been able to establish partnerships with a broad range of 400 organizations and provide technical support to promote women in business.[55]

314. More recently, employers' organizations of large establishments have begun to pay some attention to strategies aimed at increasing women's membership of representative associations. The ILO is currently working with national employers' organizations in 13 countries in the Asia-Pacific region to help them promote women's entrepreneurship and raise representation for women entrepreneurs (see box 2.1).

Minority entrepreneurs

315. Employers' organizations can contribute to the fight against racial discrimination by encouraging membership of business owners from disadvantaged racial groups. Business South Africa (BSA), a **South African** national confederation of multiracial business/employer organizations, illustrates this. Established in 1994, Business South Africa aims to represent and advance the common interests of its multiracial membership, while respecting distinct identities and needs. The development of links between small, medium and large enterprises is considered key to achieving benefits for the economy as a whole.

---

[52] P. Kantor: *Promoting women's entrepreneurship development based on good practice programmes: Some experiences from the North to the South*, Boosting Employment through Small Enterprise Development, Working Paper No. 9 (Geneva, ILO, 2001).

[53] L. Mayoux: *Jobs, gender and small enterprises: Getting the policy environment right*, Boosting Employment through Small Enterprise Development, Working Paper No. 15 (Geneva, ILO, 2001), p. 3.

[54] A.S. Davis: "Women in business: A call to action", in *Economic Reform Today: Organizing for success: Women's Business Associations*, No. 2, 1997, available at http://www.cipe.org/publications/fs/ert/e24/Davise24.htm

[55] CIPE: *Organizing for success: Strengthening women's business organizations*, available at http://www.cipe.org/programs/women/confpage.htm

Box 2.1

Some experiences on the promotion of women entrepreneurs through employers' organizations in the Asia-Pacific region

The Bangladesh Employers' Federation (BEF) has been providing training programmes for women entrepreneurs in skills development, basic bookkeeping and marketing, among others. In the framework of the ILO project on Promotion of Women in Private Sector Activities through Employers' Organizations, BEF organized seminars on equal employment opportunities policies and on gender sensitization and translated into Bengali the Bureau for Employers' Activities' guidelines for employers on gender equality. [1] The ratification of Convention No. 100 during the course of the project can be attributed in part to the advocacy activities of BEF. A national workshop on Women's Entrepreneurship Development: Women in Business, organized by BEF in collaboration with the ILO in 1993, paved the way for the establishment of the Women Entrepreneurs' Association (WEA). The WEA has organized a number of activities for women entrepreneurs, including training programmes on entrepreneurship development and networking with sister organizations in India and Nepal.

Since 1992, the Employers' Federation of Pakistan (EFP) has undertaken a number of action-oriented programmes in support of small enterprise development for women, including training programmes on Start and Improve Your Business, targeting women entrepreneurs and especially those in rural areas, translation into Urdu, dissemination of the ILO trainer's manual *Entrepreneurship development for women*, and the establishment of an Advisory Cell for Women (ACW) within EFP.

[1] ILO: *As one employer to another ... What's all this about equality? Guidelines for employers on equality at work* (Geneva, 1996).

Sources: S.D. Barwa: *ILO Asia-Pacific Regional Meeting on Promoting Women's Entrepreneurship through Employers' Organizations*, Background paper (Geneva, ILO, 2002), pp. 22-24, 53-54; and ILO: *Promotion of women in private sector activities through employers' organizations*, Progress and final evaluation report, doc. INT/95/M03/NOR (Geneva, 1999).

316. Entrepreneurs from different ethnic/racial backgrounds can also create employment for disadvantaged youth, especially from ethnic minorities, who seek a job or an entrepreneurship, but have difficulty entering the labour market. In Augsburg, **Germany**, since 1998, the Association for Foreign Entrepreneurs to Initiate Entrepreneurship, the Chamber of Industry and Commerce of Augsburg/Schwaben, the Bavarian Ministry of Labour, the German Federal Labour Office and the local labour office have cooperated on a project to involve ethnic minority-owned businesses in the apprenticeship system, while raising the employability of young people from ethnic minorities. [56] This experience is being replicated in other German cities.

Voice and representation is key to eliminating poverty and social exclusion

317. The organization of women-only groups has often been a necessary strategy to combat the distinct forms of social and economic exclusion and discrimination that low-income women face because of their sex. Women-only groups can help to build a new collective and independent identity as workers that differs from that ascribed to them by circumstance of birth, marriage or motherhood. These groups assist in bridging the gap between poor women and

Women-only groups to bridge the gap

---

[56] G. Shaw: *Ethnic minority employment through partnership: Towards a model of good practice* (Copenhagen, The Copenhagen Centre, 2002), pp. 64-65.

social networks that transcend kinship relations and open new opportunities and choices.[57] The visibility and legitimacy gained through organizing for economic and social goals can also translate into women's greater political representation. Women's membership in a representative workers' organization increases the likelihood of their exerting control over their earnings with empowering effects.[58]

318. The organization of other discriminated-against groups, such as indigenous and tribal peoples, in many regions of the world has been key to the recognition of their rights as distinct peoples and as full citizens of the countries in which they reside. Their organization has also proven effective in obtaining a fairer share in the benefits of development, as well as in bringing to a halt unwanted outside development interventions.[59]

Collective bargaining: A conduit to equality?

Equality concerns – not a separate agenda

319. The inclusion or absence of non-discrimination and/or equality clauses in collective agreements is a good indicator of the commitment of social partners to the elimination of discrimination in the workplace. Equality concerns, however, must permeate the entire collective bargaining process and not be seen as a separate agenda.

320. The reference in collective agreements to anti-discrimination national law and, wherever appropriate, relevant international standards, contributes to the enforcement of the law, especially where its application is lax, or to the safeguard of rights that might be challenged by changes in government. It allows for resolution of complaints through the grievance procedure, which is quicker and less costly than litigation. Collective bargaining can also pave the way for further progress in the legal protection of workers' rights.[60] The law may explicitly encourage or require social partners to adopt positive action measures, thus challenging the assumption that the legislative framework is sufficient for eliminating discrimination.

321. The Equal Employment Opportunity Act No. 2001-397, adopted in **France** in 2001, provides an obligation for employers to promote equal opportunities for men and women, including through collective bargaining. Following the adoption of the 2001 Act, 2,500 contracts to promote the employment of women in jobs where they are under-represented – *contrats pour la mixité des emplois* – have been negotiated.[61]

Global campaign on pay equity

322. Public Services International (PSI) has launched a global campaign on pay equity, which is due to continue throughout 2003. The campaign aims to have pay equity issues incorporated in collective bargaining by member trade unions, as part of a wider development agenda addressing poverty reduction. In partnership with the ILO, national surveys on pay equity, followed by other research initiatives and capacity-building programmes for trade unionists, were carried out in **Argentina**, **Latvia**, **Namibia** and the **Philippines**. A re-

---

[57] ILO: *Gender, poverty and employment: A reader's kit*, op. cit.

[58] S. Dasgupta: *Organizing for socio-economic security in India*, InFocus Programme on Socio-Economic Security, Discussion Paper No. 31, forthcoming (Geneva, ILO, 2002).

[59] M. Tomei: *Indigenous peoples and oil development: Reconciling conflicting interests*, Sectoral Activities Programme, Working Paper No. 123 (Geneva, ILO, 1998).

[60] M. Rueda-Catry, J.M. Supúlveda-Malbrán and M.L. Vega-Ruiz: *Tendencias y contenidos de la negociación colectiva: Fortalecimiento de las organizaciones sindicales de los países andinos* [Trends and content of collective bargaining: Strengthening trade union organizations in the Andean countries], Working Paper No. 88 (Lima, ILO, 1988).

[61] Report presented by the Government of France in October 2001 to the Committee of Experts on the Application of Conventions and Recommendations on Convention No. 111 under article 22 of the ILO Constitution.

source package on pay equity[62] has been produced to help public service trade unions, particularly in developing countries, to develop pay equity initiatives and strategies, and to build trade unions' capacity in this area so that pay equity can be used for mobilizing and organizing women in the unions. This pay equity campaign is part of a broader programme of action by PSI on equality, equity and diversity, starting in 2002 and continuing until 2007, to achieve equality for women, who represent 65 per cent of the international union's membership.

Gender equality bargaining: What have we learnt?

323. The question of collective bargaining and gender equality has received considerable attention over the past years. Experiences in gender equality bargaining can provide valuable insights to orient social partners in the fight against discrimination on grounds other than sex (see box 2.2).

324. The stage of economic development of a country and the national status of social dialogue are important determinants of the type of gender equality clauses incorporated in collective agreements and of related monitoring mechanisms. Even among industrialized countries, such as the Member States of the European Union, the extent and ways in which gender equality concerns are taken into account varies.[63] Some commonalities exist, however, in respect of the issues subject to negotiation. They generally include positive action, parental leave, flexible working hours, pay equity and, more recently, sexual harassment. Public service trade unions rely on gender-neutral evaluation of jobs to reveal inequalities in remuneration and to negotiate more persuasively the inclusion of pay equity clauses in collective agreements.[64]

Gender equality clauses in collective agreements

325. In developing countries, collective agreements are often either silent or deal with gender equality concerns in a very narrow fashion.[65] In Asia and Africa, the scope of collective bargaining is generally limited as the majority of the workforce, especially women, is employed in sectors or occupations that fall outside the realm of collective bargaining.

326. The situation in several Latin American countries[66] appears a little more favourable in this respect. An ILO study revealed that all collective agreements reviewed include, on average, around four clauses on women workers' rights, the majority relating to maternity protection rights. The content of many of these clauses goes beyond what the national law requires in this domain. A small number of clauses also provide, although in very general terms, equal opportunities for women workers.[67]

327. Trade unions alone or social partners together with the government may take joint initiatives to encourage the inclusion of gender equality issues in social and employment agendas. For example, in the **Republic of Korea**, the Federation of Korean Trade Unions (FKTU) and the Korean Confederation of Trade Unions (KCTU) have provided collective bargaining guidelines in this respect to their affiliates.

---

[62] J. Pillinger, op. cit.

[63] See L. Dickens: *Equal opportunities and collective bargaining in Europe. 4. Illuminating the process* (Luxembourg, Office for Official Publications of the European Communities, 1998).

[64] J. Pillinger, op. cit.

[65] G. Jolidon: *La lutte contre la discrimination dans l'emploi et la profession par le biais des conventions collectives de travail* [Combating discrimination in employment and occupation through collective labour agreements], Paper prepared for the InFocus Programme on Promoting the Declaration (Geneva, ILO, 2001).

[66] These include Argentina, Brazil, Chile, Paraguay, Uruguay and Venezuela.

[67] ILO: *Panorama Laboral 2002* [2002 Labour Overview] (Lima, 2002), pp. 70-78.

Box 2.2

Factors conducive to gender equality bargaining

External/environmental factors

- Good economic situation.
- Labour market conditions such as feminization, demographic change, actual or anticipated skills shortage.
- Legal framework:
  - legislation effectively promoting and supporting union organization and collective bargaining;
  - legislative equality framework.
- State encouragement or support.
- Monitoring or guidance by equality bodies

Within trade unions

- Union's concern for widening trade union membership among women.
- Women's proportion and voice in the union.
- Women's power within the union.
- Commitment of union's representatives (men and women) to equality.
- Importance attached by unions to equality bargaining.
- Internal women's or equality structures and policies.
- Women's participation in the collective bargaining process and, particularly, in negotiation.
- Equality training for both men and women.
- Bargaining training for women.
- Construction of shared interests (e.g. making a link between low pay and gender inequality in pay).

Among employers

- Concern about present or desired image of the organization.
- Significant proportion of women workers in the workforce.
- Equality measures as part of efficient management and full utilization of human resources.
- Linking equality to business interests.

Sources: ILO: *Promoting gender equality: A resource kit for trade unions. Booklet 2: Promoting gender equality through collective bargaining* (Geneva, 2002); L. Dickens: *Equal opportunities and collective bargaining in Europe. 4. Illuminating the process* (Luxembourg, Office for Official Publications of the European Communities, 1998); and S. Olney, E. Goodson, K. Maloba-Caines and F. O'Neill: *Gender equality: A guide to collective bargaining* (Geneva, ILO, 1998).

328. The general absence of equality clauses or their limited character could reflect the more general crisis that collective bargaining is undergoing, as an institution able to reconcile production and productivity goals with concerns of social redistribution. The negotiation agenda seems to be polarized between labour's demands for job security and the defence of real wages, on the one hand, and management's requirements for more flexibility, on the other.[68]

Bargaining capacity of the labour movement is significant

329. Neither the female/male ratio of the workforce nor the proportion of workers belonging to a particular racial group compared to the mainstream group seem to be key determinants of the inclusion of equality provisions in the collective bargaining process. It is rather the bargaining capacity of the labour movement that proves to be significant (see box 2.2).

[68] ibid.

330. The probability that gender equality issues are addressed and the range and type of questions that are likely to be negotiated strongly influence whether bargaining occurs at the central, sectoral or enterprise level. Centralized bargaining has traditionally tended to favour equality concerns. In the **United Kingdom,**[69] and in **Australia** and **New Zealand,**[70] the decentralization of the industrial relations framework has had a negative impact on bargaining for gender equality, particularly for equality in remuneration.

Equality bargaining beyond gender

331. The link between collective bargaining and other forms of equality has not been explored as fully as the relationship between collective bargaining and gender. There is some evidence to suggest that progress is also being made on other fronts. An ILO review found that, besides sex, race was among the grounds more frequently covered by collective agreements.[71] Further grounds comprise disability, sexual orientation, age and HIV/AIDS. In **South Africa**, the National Union of Mineworkers and Gold Fields, the second-largest producer of gold in the country, have reached a comprehensive agreement envisaging prevention programmes, voluntary testing and medical care and treatment of workers affected by HIV/AIDS. In **Ireland**, the three-year tripartite national agreement (Programme for Prosperity and Fairness), negotiated in March 2000, includes a series of provisions to facilitate access to employment of people with disabilities.[72] In **Germany**, sectoral level agreements have been negotiated to protect older workers against dismissal, while company-level agreements have provided for job accommodation measures for older workers with physical disabilities.

Enterprises mobilizing for equality

332. The effectiveness of company-level equality strategies depends to some extent on whether employers and managers believe that promoting equality pays off. This explains the growing attention to empirically ascertaining the link between equality and productivity. If the benefits outweigh, or are at least equivalent to, the costs associated with the introduction of equal opportunity or positive action policies, then employers would be clearly interested in promoting these measures.

333. The business case for equality is the rationale underpinning the management of diversity approach. This argues that the growing heterogeneity of the workforce in terms of age, gender and ethnic background, is an asset rather than a burden. The globalization of markets and production requires people from different backgrounds to satisfy the changing customer base[73] and to innovate and raise productivity. It is in the employer's self-interest to value a

The business case for equality

---

[69] L. Dickens: *Collective bargaining and the promotion of equality: The case of the United Kingdom*, Interdepartmental Projects and Activities, Working Paper No. 12 (Geneva, ILO, 1993); and J. Rubery (ed.): *Equal pay in Europe? Closing the gender wage gap* (Basingstoke, MacMillan, 1998).

[70] S. Hammond and R. Harbridge: "The impact of decentralized bargaining on women: Lessons for Europe from the Antipodes", in B. Fitzpatrick (ed.): *Bargaining in diversity: Colour, gender and ethnicity* (Dublin, Oak Tree Press, 1997).

[71] G. Jolidon, op. cit.

[72] European Industrial Relations Observatory (EIRO) Online: *Workers with disabilities: Law, bargaining and the social partners*, box 2, available at http://www.eiro.eurofound.ie/2001/02/study/TN0102201S.html

[73] "Diversity is an integral part of our business ... we actively seek new ways to better understand the diverse communities in which we operate ... that our customers and employees have different needs and aspirations." See http://www.lloydstsb.com/about_us/ltsb/company/equal_opportunities/

diverse workforce and to attract and retain the best-qualified workers from all segments of society. From this perspective, diversity management becomes an integral part of human resources management policies to create a work culture in which each employee, without any distinction based on age or disability, can develop fully his or her talents, thus contributing to overall business performance and leading to a long-term mutually rewarding relationship.[74]

334. A steadily growing number of large companies and multinational enterprises (MNEs) in **Australia**, **Canada**, **South Africa**, the **United Kingdom**, the **United States** and Europe, are adopting a diversity management approach to improve competitiveness.[75] About three-quarters of the United States-based MNEs have adopted diversity management strategies and 92 per cent of American human resource executives believe that there exists a positive correlation between these management strategies and profitability.[76] Common types of diversity management practices comprise efforts to reach out to a diverse group of students prior to and during recruitment, internship programmes involving students from minority groups, training that addresses the specific concerns of distinct groups of employees, mentoring programmes that connect members of under-represented groups placed in different hierarchical positions, and communication strategies aimed at disseminating diversity management practices both internally and to the outside world.

335. For example, in high ethnic minority areas, Lloyds TSB places posters in relevant local languages to advertise job vacancies and advertises its graduate recruitment programme in ethnic minority press. The equal opportunity policy of AT&T offers maximum opportunity for all minority and women-owned businesses to participate as its suppliers, contractors and subcontractors of goods and services.[77] General Mills has a co-mentoring programme organized by its Women's Forum, which pairs women with higher-up women for mentoring to encourage sharing experiences as a means to help them to understand the skills and competencies required for advancing in the organization.[78]

Business case arguments   336. Business case arguments have more relevance for some enterprises than for others, depending on the competitive strategy they pursue (whether it is driven by quality/innovation or by cost cutting), the labour market position or the current workforce composition. The employees who tend to benefit the most from equal opportunity policies, especially when these are voluntary, are those in an already relatively strong bargaining position. The business case agenda is not concerned about low pay or revaluing work at the bottom of the pay and occupational structures. It is the "glass ceiling" rather than the "sticky floor" that is the target of diversity management.[79]

---

[74] N. Rogovsky and E. Sims: *Corporate success through people: Making international labour standards work for you* (Geneva, ILO, 2002), p. 28.

[75] Currently, the arguments about the gains stemming from managing diversity are more common in the United States than in Europe. However, in the United States, although diversity management recognizes also the need to tackle the gender biases in current workplace practices and behaviour, in practice, the emphasis is on valuing ethnic diversity.

[76] Data from the Credit Union Executive Newsletter cited in J.L. Brant: *The business case for non-discrimination and diversity management*, Paper prepared for the Management and Corporate Citizenship Programme (Geneva, ILO, 2002), p. 4.

[77] AT&T: *Equal opportunity/affirmative action*, available at http://www.att.com/hr/life/eoaaa/index.html .

[78] J.L. Brant: *The business case for non-discrimination and diversity management*, op. cit., p. 26.

[79] J. Storey: "Equal opportunities in retrospect and prospect", in *Human Resource Management Journal* (Alexandria, VA, The Society for Human Resource Management), Vol. 9, No. 1, 1999, pp. 5-19.

The challenge of small and medium-sized enterprises

337. Many large companies still fail to see the link between non-discrimination and equality, on the one hand, and quality management and productivity, on the other. Equal opportunity policies are still largely conceived as an add-on concern, rather than instrumental to the pursuance of businesses' core objectives. Reservations about the effectiveness and cost implications of implementing equal opportunity measures are recurrent and widespread concerns. This is even more so in the case of small and medium-sized enterprises (SMEs).

Equal opportunity policies

338. An enterprise-level survey conducted by the ILO in the Caribbean in 2001 within the context of the ILO Programme for the Promotion of Management-Labour Cooperation (PROMALCO) in the Caribbean, confirmed the existence of a correlation between small size of business and the absence of a formal policy on equal opportunities. Over 350 workplaces across the Caribbean, with ten or more employees and involved in all types of activities, participated in the survey. More than 30 per cent of the surveyed workplaces reported having a formal written equal opportunity policy. Workplaces without a policy were predominantly small.[80]

339. The majority of the workplaces that claimed to have a written policy did not have any system in place to measure the impact of equal opportunity measures; nonetheless, they provided anecdotal evidence of some effects. Among these, enhanced awareness and improved workers' morale ranked the highest. It is worth noting that almost a quarter of responding enterprises with a written equal opportunity policy reported that the policy had "structural" impacts, such as changes in organizational procedures and practices.[81]

340. Further research, carried out in preparation for this Global Report, reveals interesting findings on the incidence of enterprise practices in combating discrimination and promoting equal opportunities and their effect on productivity in SMEs in two developed countries, **Australia** and the **United Kingdom**, that have had anti-discrimination legislation for several decades. In both countries, the incidence of written equal opportunities policies in SMEs is relatively high and similar (32 per cent in the **United Kingdom** and 37 per cent in **Australia**), although much lower relative to larger enterprises (83 per cent and 90 per cent, respectively). It is striking to note that almost half of the SMEs in the **United Kingdom** considered it unnecessary to adopt a formal equal opportunity policy.[82]

341. The existence of a written policy does not necessarily translate into equal opportunity practices. About 20 per cent of SMEs in both countries claim to provide facilities for workers with disabilities; however, other equal opportunity practices are only present in about 10 per cent or less of SMEs in both countries. The existence of a formal policy, however, enhances the chances of SMEs adopting equal opportunity practices.

342. In the **United Kingdom**, equal opportunity SMEs tended to be more productive, more unionized and have fewer low-paid workers and a more diverse workforce relative to other SMEs. In **Australia**, equal opportunity policies were more evenly spread across SMEs of different characteristics. In the **United Kingdom**, where positive action measures were voluntary, companies that adopted equality plans were already successful in a number of ways. In **Australia**, the law is more demanding regarding the adoption of

[80] ILO: Programme for the promotion of Management-Labour Cooperation (PROMALCO): *Caribbean enterprises survey 2001: Preliminary Findings* (Geneva, 2001).

[81] ibid.

[82] V. Pérotin, A. Robinson and J. Loundes: *Equal opportunities practices and performance*, op. cit.

equality plans, which may explain the even spread of these plans, irrespective of enterprise characteristics. This argues for public policy in this domain. A major finding was that in both countries there was no evidence of an equal opportunity policy having a negative impact on productivity.

343. Unilateral employer initiatives are important but also need to be backed by complementary means. Selective state action in non-discrimination/equality laws and beyond and joint regulation by employers and trade unions, through equality bargaining, are essential to bring about change.

Beyond national initiatives and national actors

Cooperation and alliances

344. Cooperation and alliances by trade unions or employers' organizations with representatives of civil society such as parliamentarians, human rights advocates or women's organizations help to raise the profile of equality concerns pertaining to the world of work in the media and with the public at large. They intensify pressure for policy change and are instrumental for expertise sharing and capacity building. Multi-party coalitions have also proven to be crucial in stimulating changes in the performance of economic actors operating globally.

Implementation and verification of codes of conduct

345. Since the end of the Cold War, the power of multinational enterprises has been rising while the role of the State has been receding. This has led trade unions, NGOs, women's and other non-governmental associations to join forces to influence corporate behaviour and ensure the respect of the fundamental principles and rights at work, including the principle of the elimination of discrimination.[83] An example of this is the Ethical Trading Initiative (ETI), a partnership of trade unions, NGOs and companies, supported in part by the Government of the **United Kingdom**. ETI provides a forum for the exchange of information on the implementation and the verification of codes of conduct. One of the novelties of ETI lies in its focus on verification. This involves checking on code compliance and running an implementation system for code compliance that includes defining standards and rules for the verification system adopted by a company and providing training and qualifications for those who implement it.[84]

346. This verification system appears to be more legitimate and effective than the "independent monitoring" by independent persons or organizations such as NGOs or private auditing companies hired by multinationals to assess compliance with their own codes of conduct. The "independence" and technical expertise of the monitors have been frequently questioned.[85] Another major concern is the absence in several codes of conduct of an explicit reference to the fundamental international labour standards.[86] Some analysts argue that there exist more "reliable" voluntary codes, such as the ILO *Tripartite Declaration of Principles concerning Multinational Enterprises and Social Policy* and the OECD *Guidelines for multinational enterprises*, revised in June 2000,

---

[83] UNIFEM: *Progress of the world's women: UNIFEM biennial report* (New York, 2000).

[84] ICFTU: *A trade union guide to globalisation* (Brussels, 2001).

[85] ibid.

[86] ICFTU has observed that almost all of the companies adopting the new codes operate in sectors where most workers do not belong to trade unions and in countries where trade union rights are not respected. ICFTU contends that if discrimination against trade union membership was eliminated and freedom of association and the effective recognition of the right to collective bargaining were truly respected, there might be little need for codes of conduct. See: ICFTU: *A trade union guide to globalisation*, op. cit., p. 141. The guide is also available at http://www.icftu.org/pubs/globalisation . See also Working Party on the Social Dimensions of the Liberalization of International Trade: *Overview of global developments and Office activities concerning codes of conduct, social labelling and other private sector initiatives addressing labour issues*, Governing Body doc. GB.273/WP/SDL/1(Rev.1), 273rd Session, Geneva, Nov. 1998.

Box 2.3

Discrimination is everybody's business: A corporate-led initiative in the framework of the Global Compact

Discrimination is everybody's business is a corporate-led initiative in the framework of the Global Compact launched at the World Conference against Racism, Racial Discrimination, Xenophobia and Related Intolerance, held in Durban in 2001. It aims to highlight and promote good practice on diversity in the workplace. Six companies from five continents were involved: the Swedish car manufacturer, Volvo Car Corporation; the Brazilian multimedia giant, Globo; the Indian information technology company, Satyam; the South African energy utility, Eskom and the South African financial services group, Sanlam; and the American car manufacturer, Ford Motor Company.

As a follow-up, a group of Swedish companies, NGOs and trade unions, in cooperation with Swedish government agencies, are implementing a national project designed to combat discrimination and promote diversity in the workplace. Based on the experience gained in Sweden, similar initiatives are envisaged in other countries.

Source: The Global Compact Executive Office and Volvo Car Corporation: *Discrimination is everybody's business* (2001), available at http://www.respecteurope.com/eng/news_e.html

which are anchored in a framework of universal principles that international business, governments and trade unions alike have pledged to support.[87]

347. Nevertheless, since the provisions of corporate codes of conduct extend to employees of the company's suppliers and subcontractors, they could potentially help to ensure equality of opportunities and treatment along the value chain nationally and internationally. For this to happen, codes of conduct must not become substitutes for national or international law, nor must they be used to avoid trade unions and collective bargaining. To encourage the adoption of codes of conduct that fit these requirements, Public Services International (PSI) has laid down a set of standards, known as the PSI Water Code, to which both private and public water companies should adhere with the double goal of avoiding the exploitation and unfair treatment of workers and ensuring the provision of safe drinking water and proper sanitation.

348. The Global Compact is also an example of the recognition of the key role of business in promoting fundamental human rights and the value of multistakeholder partnerships. This Compact is a values-based platform involving governments, companies, trade unions and the United Nations system and it provides a complementary framework for voluntary initiatives at the company level. The Global Compact is designed to promote institutional learning by identifying and disseminating good practices based on nine principles, which cover human rights, the fundamental principles and rights at work and environmental concerns (see box 2.3).

---

[87] International Council of Human Rights Policy (ICHRP): *Beyond voluntarism: Human rights and the developing international legal obligations of companies* (Geneva, 2002).

Part IV. Towards an action plan to eliminate discrimination at work

1. The way forward

Defining the needs for further action by the ILO

349. The purpose of the Global Report under the follow-up to the ILO Declaration on Fundamental Principles and Rights at Work is to serve as a basis for assessing the effectiveness of the assistance provided by the Organization and for determining priorities, in the form of action plans for technical cooperation. The Report is submitted to the Conference for tripartite discussion, and it will be for the Governing Body to draw conclusions from that discussion concerning the priorities and plans of action for technical cooperation to be implemented for the following four-year period.[1]

Purpose of the Global Report

350. Beyond the focus of Conventions Nos. 100 and 111 on equal remuneration and the elimination of discrimination, one fundamental aim of all ILO labour standards is to ensure that individuals and groups are treated equally in the labour market. To achieve this, the ILO promotes gender equality, more and better jobs for women, the removal of barriers to employment and training, equal treatment of migrant workers and the rights of indigenous and tribal peoples.

351. Proposals of action as follow-up to this Global Report on the elimination of discrimination in respect of employment and occupation will need to build on existing activities and to identify what can be done better and more effectively. An action plan for the elimination of discrimination at work must be aligned with the strategic objectives and the promotion of decent work. The Decent Work Agenda provides a framework that allows the linkages between patterns of discrimination in the various different societies to be recognized and a comprehensive response to be formulated. Action at the national level must be supported to facilitate the efforts of the tripartite constituents to find appropriate responses and solutions.

An action plan for the elimination of discrimination at work

352. Three main lines of action can be envisaged. First, where work has already been carried out, the priority should be the advice and dissemination of information and experience to make this work, as well as its results, better known. Also, interaction both between the ILO and the constituents and between the ILO and the other actors in the multilateral system should be

Three main lines of action

---

[1] ILO: *Declaration on Fundamental Principles and Rights at Work and its Follow-up*, International Labour Conference, 86th Session, Geneva, 1998.

facilitated. Second, ILO action should be strengthened in the areas where the Report has identified particularly important needs or gaps. Third, there should be targeted efforts to strengthen the capacity of member States and employers' and workers' organizations to deal with the multiple facets of discrimination.

Three strategies to set the wheels in motion

353. This Global Report has illustrated that when we address discrimination at work, we deal simultaneously with a number of moving targets, some of which overlap. When societies move from ignorance or denial of different forms of discrimination to awareness of them, they seek to remedy the situations that they have identified. Societies identify discrimination through the prism of their conceptual framework, based on knowledge available to them and on prevailing attitudes. To remedy it, they use the institutions and mechanisms available for addressing discrimination, and they harness political will and social mobilization to provide the necessary impetus to reach the target of eliminating discrimination and promoting equality of opportunity at work.

354. An effective plan of action should cover all these areas and should focus on strengthening knowledge, advocacy and services.

Knowledge

Equality at work indicators

355. Building, expanding, updating and disseminating the knowledge base on discrimination and equality of opportunity is a major area of work for the ILO. The continuing gap between the principle of equality at work and the reality of discrimination must be better understood. Equality at work indicators could be developed, as components of decent work indicators, to provide more adequate tools to measure progress and identify setbacks in the promotion of equality.

The link between discrimination and poverty

356. This Report has illustrated that discrimination is a factor in determining the prospects of individuals and groups. In addition, certain groups of people suffer from the compounded effects of discrimination on a number of grounds. People who suffer multiple discrimination also experience multiple disadvantage. So far, anti-poverty programmes and strategies have not automatically addressed the link between poverty and systemic discrimination. There is a need to recognize that poverty is experienced and reproduced in different ways, depending on the personal and social traits of the individuals concerned.

357. The ILO focuses on the link between employment and poverty reduction. Where discrimination sustains and shapes poverty, effective anti-poverty policy and action must tackle discrimination. Work-related policies and labour market institutions that are based on freedom from discrimination while targeting poverty and set within a growth-oriented framework would be a distinctive ILO contribution to a rights-based approach to development and poverty reduction. With a sound knowledge base on these issues, the ILO would be in a stronger position to address them in various initiatives, such as the Poverty Reduction Strategy Papers and the United Nations Development Assistance Framework processes, and in various forums. In so doing, the ILO would assume its responsibility for guiding international action in the areas that important world conferences such as those held in Beijing, Copenhagen and Durban have assigned to it.

Road maps for the elimination of discrimination at work

358. It is essential to be aware of the different forms of discrimination. For instance, a society may progress from lack of awareness or denial of some forms of discrimination to taking comprehensive action against them, but may

not, or at least not yet, be aware of or ready to address others. Governments and the social partners need to determine where they stand with regard to recognizing and addressing discrimination on different grounds, and to draw up "road maps" to help progress towards the elimination of discrimination at work. The ILO should be able to provide assistance when and where it is needed.

359. The Report has explored at some length the inequalities in remuneration between women and men that arise out of a combination of factors, such as differences in the gender division of labour and in women's career orientation, family-related factors, occupational segregation and wage structures. It could be said that the true test of an equal opportunity policy is the way it succeeds in addressing pay inequalities.

Achieving equal remuneration

360. The ILO has played a key role in placing equal remuneration on international and national agendas. The large number of ratifications of Convention No. 100 as well as broad policy statements made at the highest levels confirm this. However, there is a long way to go before equal remuneration is achieved. The time is ripe to renew the commitment to achieve equal remuneration, focusing on employing new techniques and compiling data for comparing jobs and pay, within a broader wages policy context.

361. It is necessary to document the extent of discrimination in remuneration across sectors (both formal and informal), occupations, enterprises and countries, and to produce relevant and reliable statistics on a regular basis. In this way, we can assess the real extent of discrimination in remuneration at work on the basis of sex, race and national origin, among other reasons. While the most effective strategies for equal remuneration will depend on national situations, there needs to be an assessment of the relative roles and strengths of a policy mix that includes minimum wages and/or other forms of public policy, wage negotiations and other policy measures. Job audits and evaluation and classification methods could be used to develop an "equal pay tool-kit", within the overall context of wages and human resources policies.

Advocacy

362. A coherent and sustained information and awareness-raising policy is needed to counter the negative images and suffering of groups who are discriminated against. Countervailing, positive images and solutions need to be disseminated. Cases where discrimination has been successfully eliminated need to be publicized. Guidelines and other policy documents on non-discrimination and equality need to be disseminated.

A coherent and sustained policy

363. Campaigns should be directed at political decision-makers, in particular parliamentarians, local community groups and opinion leaders, so that they are aware of the connections between discrimination in general and the special opportunities the workplace offers for promoting equality. In addition, the rights-based approach to development and poverty alleviation, in which freedom from discrimination would be a key component, should be promoted. Initiatives must be taken at the international, national and local levels and these must be well planned to maximize visibility, impact and effectiveness.

Services

364. A regulatory framework needs to be established to define discrimination, thus contributing to recognition of it when it occurs, and to establish guidelines to ensure it is eliminated. Assistance in drafting or revising legislation on equality is thus of paramount importance, and it is a traditional ILO activity that should be not only continued but also strengthened. Likewise, it

Support for legislative action

is necessary to reach out to the judiciary and the actors who have a key position in the implementation of legislation.

Support for an institutional framework

365. Two types of action are needed to improve conformity with national legislation. Firstly, traditional labour market processes and institutions, such as employment agencies, labour inspection services, vocational training and social protection schemes, need to address equality concerns on a continuous and informed basis. Secondly, national institutions dedicated to promoting and monitoring equality need to be established or strengthened.

366. Such institutions and related processes, on governmental, bipartite, tripartite or other bases, face a number of challenges, such as limitations on their powers, lack of adequate and competent staffing and funding, and lack of data. As noted in the Report, there could be separate institutions to deal with specific grounds of discrimination, such as sex, race or the treatment of migrant workers. Alternatively, there could be one institution that addresses equality concerns more generally. The first option would allow for specialization and more in-depth treatment of each particular form of discrimination, while the second would make it easier to address more complex issues of multiple discrimination. It is clear that such institutions would need strong commitment and sustained political support if they were to be effective in tackling the challenges that exist.

367. Currently, no single facility in the ILO provides assistance in these complex institutional matters. Such a facility could be established, with two main functions. The first would be to assist the establishment and operation of different institutions with mandates relating to equality, be they governmental, tripartite or concerning the social partners. This would entail the full involvement of the Bureaux for Employers' and Workers' Activities and other relevant ILO programmes. The second would be to mainstream equality concerns in ongoing programmes of the International Labour Office. Existing activities should not be duplicated; rather, there is a need to build on the strengths of ILO action and experience to date, as described in this Report. The main goals of any new and newly focused facility would be to address adequately discrimination in the labour market and to ensure that the elimination of discrimination at work is a significant step for the elimination of discrimination in other spheres.

2. Conclusion

368. Discrimination at work affects every country, every economic sector and all types of activity. By now, its formal condemnation is universal. This is particularly true for discrimination on the basis of race or sex, where the world has moved from ignorance or denial to awareness and remedial action. Yet, progress in eliminating discrimination has been uneven, and it has not always been sustainable. New forms of discrimination have emerged: discrimination as a result of disability, including HIV/AIDS, and, with demographic trends, age discrimination. Furthermore, the quest to eliminate discrimination has taken us deeper, to the very root of the problem. While the outward manifestations of discrimination may be eliminated quite quickly, confronting and eliminating the underlying structural causes calls for a great deal more work. This is particularly true for labour markets where complex interventions are needed and where deregulation or weak public policies create new constraints.

Formal condemnation is universal

369. Governments, employers and workers and their organizations have a common responsibility to work to eliminate discrimination in the workplace. Equal access to education and training, non-discriminatory labour market institutions and processes, and equal treatment at work are crucial for people in groups that are discriminated against to aspire to and to obtain decent work. Experience has shown that awareness raising, affirmative action and sanctions against those who perpetuate discrimination will help to achieve a level playing field.

370. Considerable efforts have been made to address discrimination based on sex and to promote gender equality. This is a constant and indispensable cross-cutting theme of the ILO Decent Work Agenda. However, activities have concentrated more on removing barriers to employment and perhaps not enough on inequalities in vocational education and training and in other terms and conditions of work and employment.

371. The Report shows that the Organization, particularly through technical cooperation, has dealt with discrimination mainly by way of projects and programmes directed at specific groups at work, such as women workers, migrant workers or workers with disabilities. This work needs to continue and to be consolidated. Sufficiently bold and innovative measures will be required to overcome some of the sensitivities of dealing more comprehensively with issues such as race, political opinion, sexual preference and behaviour, and religion. At the same time, there are also other grounds of discrimination that require greater attention.

372. Discrimination at work not only reinforces but also generates poverty. Most of those who suffer from the cumulative effects of multiple discrimination are to be found among the poorest segments of the population. A viable poverty-reduction strategy calls for respect for the principles concerning the fundamental rights, including freedom from discrimination at work, and for attention to the mechanisms of entry to work.

A renewed commitment

373. This Global Report has argued that discrimination at work and its elimination concerns all of us, in one way or another, as discrimination hampers both socio-economic and individual growth. The Report has also argued that the workplace is a strategic entry point for the implementation of practical ways to prevent and to eliminate discrimination and to promote equality. The ILO constituents have a responsibility to work to eliminate discrimination in the workplace. They should – singly and jointly, and with Office assistance – take matters in hand to realize progressively the Declaration's principle of the elimination of discrimination in respect of employment and occupation. This Report can serve to stimulate a renewed commitment and a practical, focused and determined effort to bring about the elimination of discrimination at work.

Annexes

Annex 1

ILO Declaration on Fundamental Principles and Rights at Work and its Follow-up

Whereas the ILO was founded in the conviction that social justice is essential to universal and lasting peace;

Whereas economic growth is essential but not sufficient to ensure equity, social progress and the eradication of poverty, confirming the need for the ILO to promote strong social policies, justice and democratic institutions;

Whereas the ILO should, now more than ever, draw upon all its standard-setting, technical cooperation and research resources in all its areas of competence, in particular employment, vocational training and working conditions, to ensure that, in the context of a global strategy for economic and social development, economic and social policies are mutually reinforcing components in order to create broad-based sustainable development;

Whereas the ILO should give special attention to the problems of persons with special social needs, particularly the unemployed and migrant workers, and mobilize and encourage international, regional and national efforts aimed at resolving their problems, and promote effective policies aimed at job creation;

Whereas, in seeking to maintain the link between social progress and economic growth, the guarantee of fundamental principles and rights at work is of particular significance in that it enables the persons concerned to claim freely and on the basis of equality of opportunity their fair share of the wealth which they have helped to generate, and to achieve fully their human potential;

Whereas the ILO is the constitutionally mandated international organization and the competent body to set and deal with international labour standards, and enjoys universal support and acknowledgement in promoting fundamental rights at work as the expression of its constitutional principles;

Whereas it is urgent, in a situation of growing economic interdependence, to reaffirm the immutable nature of the fundamental principles and rights embodied in the Constitution of the Organization and to promote their universal application;

The International Labour Conference,

1. Recalls:

    (a) that in freely joining the ILO, all Members have endorsed the principles and rights set out in its Constitution and in the Declaration of Philadelphia, and have undertaken to work towards attaining the overall objectives of the Organization to the best of their resources and fully in line with their specific circumstances;

    (b) that these principles and rights have been expressed and developed in the form of specific rights and obligations in Conventions recognized as fundamental both inside and outside the Organization.

2. Declares that all Members, even if they have not ratified the Conventions in question, have an obligation arising from the very fact of membership in the Organization, to respect, to promote and to realize, in good faith and in accordance with the Constitution, the principles concerning the fundamental rights which are the subject of those Conventions, namely:

    (a) freedom of association and the effective recognition of the right to collective bargaining;

    (b) the elimination of all forms of forced or compulsory labour;

    (c) the effective abolition of child labour; and

    (d) the elimination of discrimination in respect of employment and occupation.

3. Recognizes the obligation on the Organization to assist its Members, in response to their established and expressed needs, in order to attain these objectives by making full use of its constitutional, operational and budgetary resources, including by the mobilization of external resources and support, as well as by encouraging other international organizations with which the ILO has established relations, pursuant to article 12 of its Constitution, to support these efforts:

    (a) by offering technical cooperation and advisory services to promote the ratification and implementation of the fundamental Conventions;

    (b) by assisting those Members not yet in a position to ratify some or all of these Conventions in their efforts to respect, to promote and to realize the principles concerning fundamental rights which are the subject of those Conventions; and

    (c) by helping the Members in their efforts to create a climate for economic and social development.

4. Decides that, to give full effect to this Declaration, a promotional follow-up, which is meaningful and effective, shall be implemented in accordance with the measures specified in the annex hereto, which shall be considered as an integral part of this Declaration.

5. Stresses that labour standards should not be used for protectionist trade purposes, and that nothing in this Declaration and its follow-up shall be invoked or otherwise used for such purposes; in addition, the comparative advantage of any country should in no way be called into question by this Declaration and its follow-up.

Annex

Follow-up to the Declaration

I. Overall purpose

1. The aim of the follow-up described below is to encourage the efforts made by the Members of the Organization to promote the fundamental principles and rights enshrined in the Constitution of the ILO and the Declaration of Philadelphia and reaffirmed in this Declaration.

2. In line with this objective, which is of a strictly promotional nature, this follow-up will allow the identification of areas in which the assistance of the Organization through its technical cooperation activities may prove useful to its Members to help them implement these fundamental principles and rights. It is not a substitute for the established supervisory mechanisms, nor shall it impede their functioning; consequently, specific situations within the purview of those mechanisms shall not be examined or re-examined within the framework of this follow-up.

3. The two aspects of this follow-up, described below, are based on existing procedures: the annual follow-up concerning non-ratified fundamental Conventions will entail merely some adaptation of the present modalities of application of article 19, paragraph 5(e), of the Constitution; and the global report will serve to obtain the best results from the procedures carried out pursuant to the Constitution.

II. Annual follow-up concerning non-ratified fundamental Conventions

A. Purpose and scope

1. The purpose is to provide an opportunity to review each year, by means of simplified procedures to replace the four-year review introduced by the Governing Body in 1995, the efforts made in accordance with the Declaration by Members which have not yet ratified all the fundamental Conventions.

2. The follow-up will cover each year the four areas of fundamental principles and rights specified in the Declaration.

B. Modalities

1. The follow-up will be based on reports requested from Members under article 19, paragraph 5(e), of the Constitution. The report forms will be drawn up so as to obtain information from governments which have not ratified one or more of the fundamental Conventions, on any changes which may have taken place in their law and practice, taking due account of article 23 of the Constitution and established practice.

2. These reports, as compiled by the Office, will be reviewed by the Governing Body.

3. With a view to presenting an introduction to the reports thus compiled, drawing attention to any aspects which might call for a more in-depth discussion, the Office may call upon a group of experts appointed for this purpose by the Governing Body.

4. Adjustments to the Governing Body's existing procedures should be examined to allow Members which are not represented on the Governing

Body to provide, in the most appropriate way, clarifications which might prove necessary or useful during Governing Body discussions to supplement the information contained in their reports.

III. Global report

A. Purpose and scope

1. The purpose of this report is to provide a dynamic global picture relating to each category of fundamental principles and rights noted during the preceding four-year period, and to serve as a basis for assessing the effectiveness of the assistance provided by the Organization, and for determining priorities for the following period, in the form of action plans for technical cooperation designed in particular to mobilize the internal and external resources necessary to carry them out.

2. The report will cover, each year, one of the four categories of fundamental principles and rights in turn.

B. Modalities

1. The report will be drawn up under the responsibility of the Director-General on the basis of official information, or information gathered and assessed in accordance with established procedures. In the case of States which have not ratified the fundamental Conventions, it will be based in particular on the findings of the aforementioned annual follow-up. In the case of Members which have ratified the Conventions concerned, the report will be based in particular on reports as dealt with pursuant to article 22 of the Constitution.

2. This report will be submitted to the Conference for tripartite discussion as a report of the Director-General. The Conference may deal with this report separately from reports under article 12 of its Standing Orders, and may discuss it during a sitting devoted entirely to this report, or in any other appropriate way. It will then be for the Governing Body, at an early session, to draw conclusions from this discussion concerning the priorities and plans of action for technical cooperation to be implemented for the following four-year period.

IV. It is understood that:

1. Proposals shall be made for amendments to the Standing Orders of the Governing Body and the Conference which are required to implement the preceding provisions.

2. The Conference shall, in due course, review the operation of this follow-up in the light of the experience acquired to assess whether it has adequately fulfilled the overall purpose articulated in Part I.

The foregoing is the ILO Declaration on Fundamental Principles and Rights at Work and its Follow-up duly adopted by the General Conference of the International Labour Organization during its Eighty-sixth Session which was held at Geneva and declared closed 18 June 1998.

IN FAITH WHEREOF we have appended our signatures this nineteenth day of June 1998.

The President of the Conference,

JEAN-JACQUES OECHSLIN.

The Director-General of the International Labour Office,

MICHEL HANSENNE.

Annex 2

Table of ratifications of ILO Conventions Nos. 100 and 111

No. 100 – Equal Remuneration Convention, 1951 (160 ratifications by 1 January 2003)

No. 111 – Discrimination (Employment and Occupation Convention, 1958 (158 ratifications by 1 January 2003)

Explanation of symbols in the table

R   Convention ratified by 1 January 2003

—   Convention not ratified by 1 January 2003

Countries	Convention No. 100	Convention No. 111
Afghanistan	R	R
Albania	R	R
Algeria	R	R
Angola	R	R
Antigua and Barbuda	–	R
Argentina	R	R
Armenia	R	R
Australia	R	R
Austria	R	R
Azerbaijan	R	R
Bahamas	R	R
Bahrain	–	R
Bangladesh	R	R
Barbados	R	R
Belarus	R	R
Belgium	R	R
Belize	R	R
Benin	R	R
Bolivia	R	R
Bosnia and Herzegovina	R	R

Countries	Convention No. 100	Convention No. 111
Botswana	R	R
Brazil	R	R
Bulgaria	R	R
Burkina Faso	R	R
Burundi	R	R
Cambodia	R	R
Cameroon	R	R
Canada	R	R
Cape Verde	R	R
Central African Republic	R	R
Chad	R	R
Chile	R	R
China	R	–
Colombia	R	R
Comoros	R	–
Congo	R	R
Costa Rica	R	R
Côte d'Ivoire	R	R
Croatia	R	R
Cuba	R	R
Cyprus	R	R
Czech Republic	R	R
Democratic Rep. of the Congo	R	R
Denmark	R	R
Djibouti	R	–
Dominica	R	R
Dominican Republic	R	R
Ecuador	R	R
Egypt	R	R
El Salvador	R	R
Equatorial Guinea	R	R
Eritrea	R	R
Estonia	R	–
Ethiopia	R	R
Fiji	R	R
Finland	R	R
France	R	R
Gabon	R	R
Gambia	R	R
Georgia	R	R
Germany	R	R
Ghana	R	R
Greece	R	R
Grenada	R	–
Guatemala	R	R
Guinea	R	R
Guinea-Bissau	R	R
Guyana	R	R
Haiti	R	R
Honduras	R	R
Hungary	R	R
Iceland	R	R

Countries	Convention No. 100	Convention No. 111
India	R	R
Indonesia	R	R
Iran, Islamic Republic of	R	R
Iraq	R	R
Ireland	R	R
Israel	R	R
Italy	R	R
Jamaica	R	R
Japan	R	–
Jordan	R	R
Kazakhstan	R	R
Kenya	R	R
Kiribati	–	–
Korea, Republic of	R	R
Kuwait	–	R
Kyrgyzstan	R	R
Lao People's Democratic Republic	–	–
Latvia	R	R
Lebanon	R	R
Lesotho	R	R
Liberia	–	R
Libyan Arab Jamahiriya	R	R
Lithuania	R	R
Luxembourg	R	R
Madagascar	R	R
Malawi	R	R
Malaysia	R	–
Mali	R	R
Malta	R	R
Mauritania	R	R
Mauritius	R	R
Mexico	R	R
Moldova, Republic of	R	R
Mongolia	R	R
Morocco	R	R
Mozambique	R	R
Myanmar	–	–
Namibia	–	R
Nepal	R	R
Netherlands	R	R
New Zealand	R	R
Nicaragua	R	R
Niger	R	R
Nigeria	R	R
Norway	R	R
Oman	–	–
Pakistan	R	R
Panama	R	R
Papua New Guinea	R	R
Paraguay	R	R
Peru	R	R

Countries	Convention No. 100	Convention No. 111
Philippines	R	R
Poland	R	R
Portugal	R	R
Qatar	–	R
Romania	R	R
Russian Federation	R	R
Rwanda	R	R
Saint Kitts and Nevis	R	R
Saint Lucia	R	R
Saint Vincent and the Grenadines	R	R
San Marino	R	R
Sao Tome and Principe	R	R
Saudi Arabia	R	R
Senegal	R	R
Seychelles	R	R
Sierra Leone	R	R
Singapore	R	–
Slovakia	R	R
Slovenia	R	R
Solomon Islands	–	–
Somalia	–	R
South Africa	R	R
Spain	R	R
Sri Lanka	R	R
Sudan	R	R
Suriname	–	–
Swaziland	R	R
Sweden	R	R
Switzerland	R	R
Syrian Arab Republic	R	R
Tajikistan	R	R
Tanzania, United Republic of	R	R
Thailand	R	–
The former Yugoslav Republic of Macedonia	R	R
Togo	R	R
Trinidad and Tobago	R	R
Tunisia	R	R
Turkey	R	R
Turkmenistan	R	R
Uganda	–	–
Ukraine	R	R
United Arab Emirates	R	R
United Kingdom	R	R
United States	–	–
Uruguay	R	R
Uzbekistan	R	R
Venezuela	R	R
Viet Nam	R	R
Yemen	R	R
Yugoslavia	R	R
Zambia	R	R
Zimbabwe	R	R

Annex 3

Table 1. Changes in some features of women's participation in the labour market — selected countries[a]

Countries	Labour force participation rates					Wage employment		
	Women			Women's minus men's rates		Women outside agriculture[b]		
	1990	2000	Change	1990	2000	1990	2000	Change
Developed								
France	57.2	61.7	4.5	-17.8	-12.7			
Greece	35.4	38.9	3.5	−30.4	−25.1	36.3	39.8	3.5
Ireland	35.7	46.0	10.3	−33.3	−24.1	41.7	46.1	4.4
Italy	35.8	35.3	−0.5	−28.4	−27.3	36.0	39.8	3.8
Netherlands	53.1	64.4	11.3	−26.9	−18.2	41.7	43.9	2.2
Portugal	49.9	52.7	2.8	−24.0	−17.5	44.5	45.8	1.3
Sweden	71.2	66.6	−4.6	−6.3	−6.8	50.5	50.6	0.1
United Kingdom	53.1	54.5	1.4	−22.3	−17.1			
Australia	51.9	53.2	1.3	−23.0	−18.8			
Canada	58.5	59.5	1.0	−17.6	−13.0	46.9	48.4	1.5
Japan	50.1	49.3	−0.8	−27.3	−27.1	38.0	40.0	2.0
United States	57.6	60.2	2.6	−18.9	−14.5			
Transition								
Hungary	47.7	45.4	−2.3	−20.1	−16.0			
Poland	57.3	49.6	−7.7	−17.3	−14.9	47.3	46.9	−0.4
Romania	54.6	56.3	1.7	−12.3	−15.1	43.0	45.5	2.5
Russian Federation	60.1	51.8	−8.3	−16.3	−15.3			
Asia								
China	73.0			−12.0				
Hong Kong, China	46.6	48.5	1.9	−32.3	−27.0			
Korea, Republic of	47.0	47.4	0.4	−27.0	−27.0	37.8	40.0	2.2
Bangladesh	65.4	55.9	−9.5	−22.6	−32.9			
India	40.3			−45.6				
Pakistan	11.3	15.2	3.9	−73.6	−67.2			

Countries	Labour force participation rates					Wage employment		
	Women			Women's minus men's rates		Women outside agriculture[b]		
	1990	2000	Change	1990	2000	1990	2000	Change
Indonesia	44.6	51.5	6.9	−38.1	−33.1			
Malaysia	45.2	44.7	−0.5	−36.7	−38.1			
Philippines	47.5	50.0	2.5	−34.3	−31.8	40.4	41.1	0.7
Singapore	50.3	51.3	1.0	−28.9	−26.2	42.5	45.4	2.9
Thailand	76.3	64.2	−12.1	−11.4	−16.1			
Caribbean								
Dominican Republic	34.1	41.4	7.3	−51.7	−45.1			
Jamaica	62.4	57.6	−4.8	−14.5	−16.0			
Trinidad and Tobago	37.9	46.6	8.7	−36.4	−28.4	35.6	39.9	4.3
Latin America								
Brazil	44.0	52.8	8.8	−40.6	−29.2	42.8	45.4	2.6
Chile	31.8	36.5	4.7	−43.3	−37.9			
Costa Rica	32.5	38.5	6.0	−50.0	−43.0	37.2	39.3	2.1
Ecuador	28.2	52.2	24.0	−53.8	−29.9			
Guatemala	28.0	45.6	17.6	−61.6	−42.3			
Mexico	21.6	38.5	16.9	−53.9	−45.3	36.5	37.3	0.8
Peru	29.3	58.1	28.8	−50.5	−21.3		33.3	
Uruguay	42.8	49.2	6.4	−24.2	−24.3			
Africa								
Ethiopia	57.9	71.9	14.0	−28.1	−17.8			
Mauritius	34.7			−45.9				
Rwanda	83.7	85.1	1.4	−9.9	−2.0			
Tanzania, United Republic of	83.4				−5.6			
South Africa	45.6	43.9	−1.7	−34.3	−13.8			
Ghana	81.8			−0.6				
Mali	72.9			−17.3				
Middle East								
Iran, Islamic Republic of	21.4	10.6	−10.8	−59.1	−64.2			
Israel	40.8	47.3	6.5	−21.5	−13.4		48.3	
Jordan	17.3	11.6	−5.7	−58.2	−52.0			
Lebanon	24.2	18.7	−5.5	−50.0	−48.6			
Saudi Arabia	14.6		−14.6	−70.1				
Syrian Arab Republic	23.6	16.7	−6.9	−54.7				
North Africa								
Egypt	26.7	19.6	−7.1	−46.5	−51.9	20.5	20.9	0.4
Morocco	38.8	30.3	−8.5	−41.2	−49.0			
Sudan	23.1	29.1	6.0	−52.1	−45.6			

Note: 1990 = data for 1990 or the closest year available; 2000 = data for 2000 or the latest year available.
[a] Labour force participation rates taken from 15+ age group, except for those for France, Malaysia and the Netherlands, which are taken from the 15-64 age group.   [b] Women's wage employment outside agriculture = women's wage employment in the non-agricultural sector as a percentage of total non-agricultural employees. This is one of the Millenium Development Goal indicators.   Blank spaces = information not available.
Sources: ILO: *Key Indicators of the Labour Market (KILM) 2001-2002* (Geneva, 2002), KILM 1; and ILO: *Labour Statistics Yearbook Database (LABORSTA)*.

Table 2. Unemployment differentials between women and men — selected countries

Countries	1990			2000			Change
	Women	Men	Women's minus men's rates	Women	Men	Women's minus men's rates	1990 to 2000
Developed							
France	12.0	7.0	5.0	11.9	8.5	3.4	−1.6
Greece	11.7	4.3	7.4	16.5	7.0	9.5	2.1
Ireland	13.8	12.6	1.2	4.6	4.8	−0.2	−1.4
Italy	17.6	7.8	9.8	15.7	8.7	7.0	−2.8
Netherlands	10.6	5.4	5.2	4.9	2.7	2.7	−2.5
Portugal	6.8	3.1	3.7	4.8	2.9	1.9	−1.8
Sweden	1.8	1.8	0	6.7	7.4	−0.7	−0.7
United Kingdom	4.8	8.3	−0.5	5.1	6.7	−1.6	−1.1
Australia	7.1	6.9	0.2	6.7	7.2	−0.5	−0.7
Canada	8.1	8.2	−0.1	6.7	6.9	−0.2	−0.1
Japan	2.2	2.0	0.2	4.5	5.0	−0.5	−0.7
United States	5.5	5.7	−0.2	4.6	3.7	0.9	1.1
Transition							
Hungary	1.4	1.8	−0.4	6.3	7.5	−1.2	−0.8
Poland	7.1	5.8	1.3	18.5	15.2	3.3	2.0
Romania	4.0	2.2	1.8	6.2	7.4	−1.2	−3.0
Russian Federation	5.2	5.2	0	13.1	13.6	−0.5	−0.5
Asia							
China	1.2	0.9	0.3				
Hong Kong, China	1.3	1.3	0	4.0	5.1	−1.1	−1.1
Korea, Republic of	1.8	2.9	−0.9	5.1	7.1	−2.0	−1.1
Bangladesh	1.9	2.0	−0.1	2.3	2.7	−0.4	
India							
Pakistan	0.9	3.4	12.3	14.9	4.2	10.7	−1.6
Indonesia							
Malaysia							
Philippines	9.8	7.1	2.7	9.9	10.3	−0.4	−3.1
Singapore	1.3	1.9	−0.6	4.6	4.5	0.1	0.7
Thailand	2.4	2.1	0.3	3.0	3.0	0	−0.3
Caribbean							
Dominican Republic	33.1	12.5	20.6	28.6	9.5	19.1	−1.5
Jamaica	23.1	9.3	13.8	22.5	10.0	12.5	−1.3
Trinidad and Tobago	24.2	17.8	6.4	16.8	10.9	5.9	−0.5
Latin America							
Brazil	3.4	3.8	−0.4	11.6	7.2	4.4	4.8
Chile	5.7	5.7	0	7.6	7.0	0.6	0.6
Costa Rica	5.9	4.2	1.7	8.2	4.9	3.3	1.6
Ecuador	9.1	4.3	4.4	16.0	8.4	7.6	3.2
Guatemala							
Mexico	4.2	2.5	1.7	2.6	1.8	0.8	−0.9

Countries	1990			2000			Change
	Women	Men	Women's minus men's rates	Women	Men	Women's minus men's rates	1990 to 2000
Peru	7.3	4.8	2.5	8.6	7.5	1.1	−1.4
Uruguay	10.9	6.9	4.0	14.6	8.7	5.9	1.9
Africa							
Ethiopia							
Mauritius							
Rwanda							
Tanzania, United Republic of	4.2	2.7	1.5				
South Africa				27.8	19.8	8	
Ghana							
Mali							
Middle East							
Iran, Islamic Republic of							
Israel	11.3	8.4	2.9	8.1	8.5	−0.4	−3.3
Jordan				20.7	11.8	8.9	8.9
Lebanon				7.2	9.0	−1.8	
Saudi Arabia							
Syrian Arab Republic	14.0	5.2	8.8				
North Africa							
Egypt	17.9	5.2	12.7	19.9	5.1	14.8	2.1
Morocco	20.4	14.2	6.2	27.6	20.3	7.3	1.1
Sudan							

Note: 1990 = data for 1990 or the closest year available; 2000 = data for 2000 or the latest year available; Blank spaces = information not available.
Source: ILO: *KILM 2001–2002* (Geneva, 2002), KILM 8.

Table 3. Index of dissimilarity (ID)[a] and gender-dominated non-agricultural occupations for selected countries

Country	Latest year	Number of occupations sampled	Number of gender-dominated occupations			Percentage of total labour force in gender-dominated occupations	Percentage of male labour force in male-dominated occupations	Percentage of female labour force in female-dominated occupations	Percentage of women in the non-agricultural labour force	ID
			Total	Women-dominated	Men-dominated					
Major Europe										
Austria	2000	71	31	3	28	53.2	53.8	10.1	43.3	0.569
France	1999	119	62	8	54	44.9	49.6	30.7	45.5	0.554
Germany	2000	80	49	8	41	53.2	48.9	37.5	43.0	0.537
Major non-Europe										
United States	2000	104	47	15	32	36.8	33.1	33.3	47.2	0.463
Central and Eastern Europe										
Poland	2001	100	47	15	32	52.1	51.9	43.8	45.3	0.616
Belarus	1999	100	43	28	15	62.3	60.1	56.1	51.1	0.647
Russian Federation	2000	30	8	5	3	35.2	33.7	29.7	48.2	0.501
Asia										
Hong Kong, China	2001	122				40.6	40.5	32.1	45.3	0.503
Korea, Republic of[b]	2000	149 (41)	75	5	70	40.7	56.0	4.9	36.1	0.549 (0.431)
Pakistan	1998	25	23	0	23	92.8	97.6	0	4.9	0.455
Thailand	2000	111	25	5	20	25.0	31.5	12.3	48.2	0.405
Middle East										
Iran, Islamic Republic of	1996	26	20	0	20	85.2	92.8	0	13.1	0.639

[a] The index of dissimilarity (ID) measures the proportion of one sex that would have to change occupations, holding employment of the other sex constant, in order to achieve gender equality in employment. The ID has values that range between 0 (no segregation, implying that there is an equal percentage of women and men in each occupation) and 1 (complete segregation, implying that all female workers are in occupations where there are no male workers). The ID is used here to illustrate the level of segregation, but it should be borne in mind that in investigating occupational segregation it is important to look at several different types of statistics.   [b] Calculations for number of occupations sampled and ID are based on two different sample sizes.   Blank spaces = information not available.

Source: R. Anker and H. Melkas: *Gender-based occupational segregation*, Background paper prepared for this fourth Global Report (Geneva, ILO, 2002). Calculations are based on occupational data from the ILO SEGREGAT database (as updated in 2002).

Table 4. Findings from selected studies using the Oaxaca-Blinder approach: Proportion of the gender pay gap (GPG) attributed to labour market discrimination[a]

Author	Country	Control variables	Key explanatory variables (in descending order)	Percentage of GPG explained by differences in characteristics	Percentage of GPG attributed to discrimination
Oaxaca (1973)	United States	12: Education, experience, number of children, class of worker, occupation (10), industry (16), health problems, part time, migration, marital status, size of urban area, region	Industry Occupation Marital status Part time Children	42% (whites) 44% (blacks) [average of two estimates]	58% (whites) 56% (blacks) [average of two estimates]
Blinder (1973)	United States	12: Age, region, education, training, occupation (8), union, veteran status, health, local labour market, mobility, length of time on job	Occupation Length of time on job Union membership	34%	66%
Asplund et al. (1993)[b]	Denmark (DK) Finland (FI) Norway (NO) Sweden (SW)	12: Experience, education, tenure, part time, cohabitation, temporary contract, immigrant, health, province, number of children, occupation (6), sector (7)	DK: Sector, occupation, experience FI: Sector NO: Sector, occupation SW: Sector, occupation, part time	DK: 28% FI: 10% NO: 34% SW: 49%	DK: 72% FI: 90% NO: 66% SW: 51%
Langford (1995)	Australia	9: School, potential experience, tertiary education field, marital status, children, country of birth, occupation (8), industry (12), public/private	Industry Tertiary education field Potential experience	51%	49%
Le Grand (1991)[b]	Sweden	21: Education, experience, seniority, immigrant, big city, married, children, housework, career interruption, positional grade, union, public sector, occupational segregation (female share), physical work, autonomy, working time inconvenience, work monotony, piece-work, commuting time, part time, hectic work	Positional grade Occupational segregation Experience	57%	43%
Plasman et al. (2001)	Belgium	11: Education, work experience, years of service in company, occupation (ISCO 2-digit), paid working hours, type of contract, unsocial hours premium, economic/financial control at company, paid overtime, sector (NACE 2-digit), company size	Sector Years of service Occupation	48%	52%

[a] The main objective of the Oaxaca-Blinder wage decomposition is to separate out the explained portion of the gender pay gap and the unexplained portion attributable to discrimination. The method relies on the following assumptions: (i) individual characteristics are the result of free choices made by individual men and women; (ii) individual characteristics can be taken as approximate measures of productivity; and (iii) productivity equals pay. Two methodological problems arise: the first problem is the choice and definition of individual variables related to productivity (some are more readily measurable than others); the second problem is "feedback" effects, i.e. gender differences in characteristics (education, experience, occupation, etc.), which may themselves reflect the impact of discrimination. Despite its drawbacks, the Oaxaca-Blinder approach has the advantage of isolating the issue of labour market discrimination and thereby facilitating a clear policy focus. [b] These studies refer to the gender pay gap as the ratio of male average pay to female average pay.

Source: D. Grimshaw and J. Rubery: *The adjusted gender pay gap: A critical appraisal of standard decomposition techniques.* Paper prepared as part of the work by the coordinating team of the Group of Experts on Gender and Employment commissioned by the Equal Opportunities Unit in the European Commission (Manchester, University of Manchester Institute of Science and Technology, 2002).